Whose Life?

Community Care of Older People and their Families

Chris Iveson

BT Press

First published in October 1990
Reprinted with corrections, February 1993
Published by Brief Therapy Press
17 Avenue Mansions, Finchley Road, London NW3 7AX

© Chris Iveson

Typeset by Alex Gollner

ISBN 1 871697 66 2

CONTENTS

ACKNOWLEDGEMENTS

This short book describes not only my work, but also the work of many colleagues with whom I have collaborated over the years. Of these the most influential have been the staff of the Home Care Team covering the Camden Town area of North London. Joy Peterson (home help organiser) set the ball rolling with her belief that no-one should be removed from his or her own home without their full consent, and it was Joy who sat it out with Mr. Walker. Bob Chard (Social Worker) led the professionals into their imaginative and effective contract with Mr. More; and it was Bob, more than anyone, who gave the status and dignity to work with older people which led to the team having such an influence over the work of the area office. It was he and Bridget Bergin (volunteer organiser) who taught themselves about 'reality orientation'. Karen Charman was the occupational therapist and Yvonne the home help organiser involved with Mr. More; while Yvonne Lewinson and another occupational therapist, Fatma Dusoruth were in the arena with Miss Kelleher. Other important contributors to the team were Larkin Colton, Richard Brayshay, Linda Barber, Sabrina Wilson, and the eighty home helps and one hundred and twenty volunteers whose flexibility and good heartedness made it all possible.

The therapist who did so well the second time round with Mrs. Young was Pauline Hudson, social worker at the Jules Thorne Day Hospital in Bloomsbury Health Authority.

AUTHOR

Chris Iveson is a social work team leader in Westminster Social Services. He is presently based at the Marlborough Family Service (an NHS children and adult psychiatric clinic). He is a member of the Institute of Family Therapy and a founder member of the Brief Therapy Practice.

He has co-authored (with Evan George and Harvey Ratner) *Problem to Solution: Brief Therapy with Individuals and Families*.

INTRODUCTION

This book is primarily a storybook – but one of true stories, give or take a few details to preserve confidentiality. They are stories about older people living alone or with their families. Some of the people are likeable, some not so likeable, but all will be familiar to anyone working regularly with older people. The stories represent the human and professional dilemmas which face us when working with people who are both vulnerable and discriminated against. They come from my work as a generic, area-based social worker, as a hospital social worker, as a home care services manager and as a counsellor. Interwoven with the stories of the clients and their carers is a story of theory building – particularly around the application of family therapy theories to work with older people. It was in fact the lack of a family therapy book on older people which spurred me to set about writing this one.

All the people kind enough to read the original draft have asked me, "Who is the book for?" I'm not sure of the answer except that it could be for all the people I have been and all those I have worked with! Social workers, occupational therapists, residential staff, home help organisers, geriatricians and everyone else with a professional interest in older people. More specifically it is aimed at anyone who would like to try out some new, and sometimes disturbing, ideas with that minority of their clients who take up the majority of their time.

Chris Iveson
October 1990

CHAPTER ONE

SOME THEORETICAL PERSPECTIVES

INTRODUCTION

Agnes and Mary had been living together for eighty-two years when I met them. Agnes had referred herself to the local Social Services office requesting residential care for her older sister. Agnes was alone when I called and began with a desperate plea for us to take her sister away before they were both driven mad! I asked to see the two sisters together and Mary was summoned into the room. There began an argument which in its form, if not its content, must have been almost as old as the women themselves. As they went round and round the well-worn track of their dispute, it slowly became clear that they were protecting as much as they were attacking each other. Agnes was not telling Mary she had to go and Mary constantly drew back from the brink of rejection of her sister. Neither wanted to admit to the other, nor perhaps to herself, that they could no longer cope with the relationship between them. The growing weakness of both and the dependency of Mary on Agnes was too much to bear but the consequences were too awful to face.

It is not uncommon for a family to call in professionals at such critical points in its life. Agnes wanted me to tell Mary she was going on holiday. I would not agree to do this and instead asked Agnes to tell her sister the truth. My view was that by the later stages of life most people have been through and survived enough to prepare them for almost anything. I also assumed that the shock of the truth was likely to be less damaging than the slow erosion of a lie. We sat around the sisters' small electric fire on that November afternoon for an hour while they accused and counter accused each other over a lifetime of memories, and all the while Agnes edged closer to the 'truth'. Then it came. Agnes said: "You can't stay here Mary; you'll have to go into a home." Mary looked incredulous; Agnes repeated her sentence with a desperate and resigned sadness. This time Mary understood and, as the truth struck home, she jerked in a violent spasm: her eyes rolled into

her head and her whole body began to shake, her face to contort
and her mouth began to froth.

It was twenty minutes before the doctor arrived. He pronounced
a serious stroke, gave only a fifty percent chance of survival,
called an ambulance and departed. Agnes and I were left with our
unshared guilt until the ambulance arrived fifteen minutes later.
The crew looked as doubtful as had the doctor and quickly
transferred the still quivering Mary to a stretcher. But before they
had quite passed through the door Mary suddenly sat bolt
upright and cried: "Where's my handbag?" She left clutching it to
her chest. A few days later she was pronounced fit with no
evidence of a stroke and moved, at her sister's wish, to a nearby
home for older people. She established herself there and for the
next few years the two sisters enjoyed an Indian summer in their
lifelong relationship.

This all happened when I was new to social work and new to
family therapy, but it is an event which served both as
confirmation and warning. The sisters *did* rise to the occasion but
the 'stroke' *might* have been real. As a family therapist I had
thought that this painful issue would be best dealt with openly
and directly by the sisters. It was clearly a relationship problem,
and it seemed the obvious way to resolve such a problem is to
bring both parties together. While this proved to be the case, I was
equally reminded that older people are more susceptible to
physical illness and might also choose to succumb to it rather than
fight on. I have no doubt that Mary came very close to death.

I saw Agnes and Mary almost twenty years ago. My final case
example (in this book) has just begun. The book will cover some
of the dilemmas, discoveries, failures and successes I have
struggled with in between. During this time I have held a number
of posts: generic social worker, area office team leader, domicillary
services manager and latterly senior social worker in a child and
family psychiatry department but based at the Marlborough
Family Service in London which takes referrals of people of all
ages. For much of this time I have practised and taught family
therapy. I write this book, therefore, not as a specialist in the
needs and treatment of older people, but as a family therapist

who has applied family therapy ideas to the day to day delivery of a wide range of services to older people. Many readers will have considerably more experience and commitment to work with older people and will undoubtedly find the book raises a number of serious questions. It does not purport to have all the answers but I hope it will be seen as a stimulus for the increasing number of specialists who work with older people to develop further the application of family therapy ideas and practices in their work.

THEORETICAL ISSUES

The work described in this book draws on a number of family therapy theories, not all of which sit well together and none of which have been fully able to resolve the dilemma posed by Agnes and Mary's position. The last chapter will describe a departure from 'mainstream' family therapy which I think in the future may prove even more productive in problem resolution and change. But for the most part a number of fundamental theories jostle with each other for space. They are not always mutually exclusive, but rest on somewhat differing principles. Each theory is, therefore, only as good as it is useful; and though each is based on a wide range of different experiences, there is always something new and something unexplained around every corner!

Systems Theory

Systems theory is a collection of ideas which from some stand points seem extraordinarily simple and obvious, while from others they appear almost beyond the capacity of the human mind to grasp. In its simplest form it states that all people and things are parts of systems, each one influencing and being influenced by the others. The usual rules of cause and effect are replaced by interrelatedness and circularity. In family terms this means no family member can act without having an influence on everyone else. The chicken and the egg become not a line stretching into infinity, but a circle in which the egg cannot exist without the chicken nor the chicken without the egg. They are interdependent. In such a situation (which might be seen as a microcosm of life) understanding of the chicken and the egg comes, as much as anything, from understanding the relationship between them.

Systems theory is concerned with just this: understanding the relationships which hold the system parts together to form the whole. Family therapy is a product of this theory and has moved the emphasis from the study of the individual (the chicken *or* the egg) to the study of what happens between individuals which keeps them acting together – the study of relationships.

'Interactional' Theories

Family therapy in part originated from ideas about communication – that in certain circumstances conflicting communications spoken and unspoken, would cause problems. A simple example would be two people talking but misunderstanding each other. If you were to listen to the middle part of such a conversation you might not make sense of it and think it was two crazy people, or you might actually work out that it is two people misunderstanding each other. What you would *not* be able to do is find a *cause* of the problem. Each person would appear equally involved, equally responsible and equally trapped. They would go on like this until such time as they got fed up and parted, or brought in a third party to help work out what was happening. This is very much a family therapist's position. No one can really know who *causes* what in a family, everything is far too complex and interrelated. But communication blocks, misunderstandings, double messages, one-sided views and hobby horses can all give rise to sometimes serious family problems. It is a family therapist's job to help the family unravel some of these communication knots so they are again able to pick up the thread of their lives. For myself I found these theories, and the techniques which derive from them, most useful when working with isolated older people with no family contact. Chapters Three and Four will illustrate how understanding some of the complexity of apparently simple communications can be a great help in working out an approach to problem solving which is both effective and user-friendly. These theories derive largely from the Mental Research Institute in Palo Alto, California and are best represented by Herr and Weakland (1979).

Structural theories

Structural family therapy was developed primarily by Salvador Minuchin. Minuchin, too, believes in open communication, but alongside this he introduces a theory about how families need to organise themselves if they are to fulfil their many functions. Put most simply, he argues that each generation should be clearly defined, with middle generation parents free from control by their own parents and fully in charge of their younger children. Where adults have not separated emotionally from their parents, Minuchin predicts family problems.

Minuchin and his colleagues also developed a characteristic style of work which involved getting family members to *have* their problem during the session rather than just talk about it. So if someone says: "He never listens to me", she might be asked to try out ways of getting herself heard there and then. This was, in fact, what I was doing with Agnes and Mary, supporting Agnes to tell to Mary in her own words what it was she had to say. No easy task and many would argue that such brutal truth is not in a client's interest.

Family Life Cycle

Ideas about the family life cycle permeate most family therapy theories and have a number of uses. Firstly, they remind us of transition points which are likely to cause stress: retirement, illness and bereavement are obvious examples. Secondly, they highlight the connections between other transitional events within the family: a young person leaving home may create more space within a family for the care of an older member or cause distress to parents which reverberates more adversely on the older person. In a later chapter one example will illustrate how a failure to take fully into account all the life cycle changes within a particular family led to the collapse of an otherwise well-thought-out care plan. Thirdly and lastly, life cycle theory can help us understand some apparently chronic problems and consider unusual ways of dealing with them. For instance, it is often thought that each life cycle stage must be satisfactorily passed for full development to occur. In one case, cited in the scant family therapy literature[1], the parents' failure to deal adequately with their two year old daughter's temper tantrums led them to continue to be 'ruled' by her thirty years later. This they managed to put up with until two other major life cycle events added to their burden and they sought help. The therapy was based on the same ideas used to deal with tantrumming two-year-olds and it worked. The parents were then free to cope with the many other issues which, as older people, they were having to face.

Solution Theory

The development of theories about solutions is likely to have a profound effect on counselling in the future. In essence it offers an entirely new direction by arguing that problems are best resolved not by understanding them, but by understanding solution processes. Finding out how a person *solves* problems is ultimately more useful than finding out how he or she got the problems in the first place. I have written about this elsewhere (George, Iveson and Ratner, 1990), but by applying these ideas specifically to older people a number of advantages are apparent. Firstly, it is an approach based on strength-enhancement, highlighting and making the most of what is already there or potentially there. Older people have enough information about their deficits, and looking at the debit side of life is rarely an uplifting pastime. Looking at achievements, skills and strengths is a booster for a person of any age, but for an older person with the end of life in sight, it is likely to be particularly empowering.

The second advantage is that this is an immediate approach which relies on the client for direction and goals. Its aim is to overcome the complaint or problem in as direct and short a time as possible. This, too, is empowering for people who are commonly expected to agree with others about what is best for them.

---

[1] Barnhill L. and Lango D., "Fixation and Regression in the Family Life Cycle" *Family Process* 17.4 (1978)

THE LIMITATIONS OF THEORY

The influence of each of these theories on my work with older people will be described and expanded in relation to case examples. What must still be remembered is that they are only theories – they are not truths. This was first brought home to me some time ago when I presented one of the cases at a workshop. In an audience of some fifty people, one face stood out as being completely in touch with what I was saying. He came up to me afterwards as if to a soul-mate and explained how what I had described perfectly fitted his theory of counselling. And it did – he might have done exactly the same as me, yet his *theory* was entirely different. This has proved to be the case over and over again and I have learned to take advantage of it. I now rarely explain how I *think* about what I do until I have heard how an audience would explain it. This way I learn new theories and audiences realise they don't need to learn mine!

This is not to say that theories are dispensable. For me they are essential and there is very little I do in counselling and related work which cannot be explained in terms of a theory. This does not mean that the theory is 'right'; it is simply a means of making sense to myself of my actions so that I can keep those which work and jettison those which don't. In some ways a theory can be seen as a road to a destination (the client's goal). For me the journey (the therapy) is not important; it is a means to arrive as quickly as possible at the destination. I will therefore use motorways. For others the journey might be seen as a part of the destination, so a more leisurely and scenic route is taken.

The value and limitation of theory is rather more elegantly stated by Umberto Eco's character in *The Name of the Rose*, William of Baskerville (based on the medieval philosopher William of Occam):

"The order that our mind imagines is like a net, or like a ladder, built to attain something. But afterwards you must throw the ladder away, because you discover that, even if it was useful, it was meaningless.... The only truths that are useful are instruments to be thrown away".

This then is a book of truths. Like William's ladders, the 'truths' or theories have provided a route to where I was aiming to go. All but the most recent have been cast aside many times only to be brought out again when other ladders did not seem up to the task in hand. Only the latest ladder, the solution ladder, has not yet been cast aside!

WORKING ASSUMPTIONS

If a theory is represented by an extending ladder, then a working assumption is rather like a step ladder – it is unable to reach the dizzy heights but is good enough for most jobs. I have a number of working assumptions most of which are challengeable and have little relationship to observable events, yet they have served their purpose well enough to be kept in constant use. They will be in evidence throughout the following chapters and it is likely that most readers will disagree strongly with at least one of them.

Older people belong

As a family therapist I think of people as belonging to systems: as being part of a whole, the whole being made up of all the parts *and the connections between them*. This is true of all people irrespective of age. It is impossible to be associated with other people and not be part of a set of interrelationships which influence all those who play a part. Obvious as this is, it is not uncommon for older people to be treated as if they are *not* part of the people associating with them. In my work as a domicillary services manager with anything up to a thousand clients, it was all too easy to regard the older person as the 'problem' and exclude him or her from the association of people providing the service. Knowing what is best for others might be an act based on the most worthy intentions, but it also implies the exclusion of the recipient from the process of knowing. Such an exclusion is ultimately a denial of human rights and so falls among those 'good' intentions which pave the road to hell! If we think 'systemically', if we acknowledge that we are all *part* of a larger whole, then it is impossible to deny the 'belongingnesss' of anyone, and older people can do nothing less than belong.

Older people are responsible

But if older people belong, if they are a part of what goes on, then they must *influence* as well as be influenced by those around them.

Systems theory is sometimes seen as a way of denying individual responsibility but it can equally be seen as understanding *shared* responsibility. If all those involved in a system whether it be a family or a group of professionals, have a part in the development of that system, a say in what goes on, they also share responsibility for what goes on.

So if older people belong if they are part of a system, they must also share responsibility for whatever is happening in their lives.

I know that many people regard this assumption as deeply flawed, and were it truly a set of step-ladders they would condemn it as dangerous.

Babies belong but can they share any responsibility for the life they lead? So what about seriously confused people? They are certainly able to influence the lives of those around them, but can they really be treated as responsible? The answer is that I don't know. I would argue that to compare older people with children is to deny the best part of a lifetime's experience, but I cannot say that I *know* the responsibility which accompanies this experience always survives the physical and mental impairment which can accompany old age. But neither can I say that it doesn't. Like the nurses who cared for my mother during her last days: they did not *know* if she could hear them through her coma, but neither did they know that she couldn't. Given this lack of certainty, they decided to act as if she could hear something, for which we as family will always be grateful. It is a similar act of faith which leads me to think of all adult people as continuing in some way to share responsibility for the events which shape their lives.

Older People Choose

With responsibility comes choice. One cannot be responsible for something over which one has no say, or in which one has no part. If older people belong and share responsibility for the events which make up their lives, they must also be making choices and be *capable of making other choices*.

This too is an act of faith. There is no way of knowing that all people retain the capacity to choose, but believing that they do

leads to one sort of behaviour and believing that they don't leads
to another.

For several years members of the home care team I managed kept
Mrs. Peebles, an apparently very confused woman in the
community on the basis that when asked about her wishes, she
would say that she wanted to be at home. She allowed minimal
support, lived in appalling conditions and frequently aroused
neighbours to extremes of anxiety. The team respected her wishes
and met several times with neighbours and other professionals to
recruit and maintain their support. Meanwhile, the client's
behaviour gradually grew more distressing and
incomprehensible. Acting on the shared belief that at some level
the client was still capable of choice, we invested in an Open
University 'reality orientation' course, and two team members
began a short daily orientation programme with Mrs. Peebles.
They found out that the client had been going off at night to meet
her husband from his night shift at Kings Cross Station. He had
been dead sixteen years. Much of the 'reality' Mrs. Peebles had to
face was therefore painful. They also found that the home in
which she thought she wanted to live had in fact been pulled
down many years ago – she did not know if she wanted to live in
her present home. Within a week of beginning this programme
(which took up one hour of staff time each weekday), the workers
had discovered that what had appeared as *confusion* about where
she wanted to live, was in fact *indecision*. She did not like where
she was but was afraid that an alternative might be worse.
Without a way to communicate her dilemma to those around her,
Mrs. Peebles was trapped.

Within two weeks of beginning the programme, the team were
more in touch with Mrs. Peebles – her history, her fears and hopes
than at any time during the previous eight years. We also found
that she had an older sister who, if still alive, would be ninety-
four. Mrs. Peebles thought her sister was in an old people's home
somewhere in North London, and in a few days the team tracked
her down. The matron was contacted with a view to the sisters
meeting and the possibility of Mrs. Peebles moving to the home.
The matron said her client was very well settled in the home and
meeting her sister might disturb her. She declined to allow a visit.

The team was not unduly put off. We were all familiar with the tendency for professionals to make decisions for their older clients, but we also knew that most professionals could be convinced that taking a different view might sometimes be worth the risk. However, time was not on Mrs. Peebles' side and while we considered a new approach to the home, she died.

Along with our anger and sadness that Mrs. Peebles' reunion with her sister had never happened went a deep sense of relief that she had at least died in a state of connection with the world, and that this connectedness had once again given her the means to express dilemmas and so consider choices. Mrs. Peebles had never lost the capacity to make choices about her place in the world, but for a time the world attempted to deny her that opportunity. And I suppose a final thought might be that once she regained her right to choose, she chose to die.

So these three assumptions are the somewhat rickety step-ladders underlying the work described in this book. On the other hand, it is clear that older people's 'belongingness', or full membership of society, their responsibility for their actions and their capacity to make choices are all seriously questionable. Many of the services available to them would appear to be based on very different principles, but, unlike the theories, these assumptions are for me unalterable: they are the bottom line of human rights.

CHAPTER 2

EMPOWERMENT NOT PROTECTION

Some years ago I was representing an elderly woman at a Social Security Appeals Tribunal. She had not been entirely open with me about her financial resources, so we lost our case. I might not have remembered it but for two things: firstly, I twisted my ankle on the stairs leading to the tribunal room and spent the entire proceedings in agony; and secondly, I was taken aback by the aside whispered to me by the victorious Social Security representative, "Once a scrounger always a scrounger!". My client was a 'dear old lady' of seventy-nine. I remembered the injustice of that remark for a very long time. It was many years before I realised the greater injustice of my own views.

Unsympathetic as the Social Security man was he had not dissociated my client from what he thought to be her past. He had not, because she had passed the age of sixty-five, begun to treat her differently than before. She was not his "dear old lady" like she was mine. Unpleasant he might have been but he also saw my client as belonging, responsible and capable of making choices. I thought she needed protection.

Vulnerability and Protection

As people become older they may well become less able to fend for themselves. Even if permitted to work, they may not have the physical or mental stamina or capacity, and in many areas of daily life the very old, in particular, may find their activities curtailed by diminishing ability. Does this mean older people need protection? In some ways it does – certainly from those who would use their greater strengths abusively. But older people also get a great deal more protection than they need. Mrs. Peebles' sister, for instance, was protected from meeting once again with her sibling of ninety years standing, and I protected my Social Security client from knowing I knew she had deceived me. In ways such as these, the protection of older people is a denial of their right to be treated as complete human beings.

During my home care team years we identified a number of ways this sort of protection operated:

a)   We protect older people from themselves by making key decisions for them. How many people have been admitted to residential care not because they want it, but because they have no answer to the charge that they fell or they wandered? Yet how many older people wandering at night come to real harm, and how difficult is it to help a person arrange accommodation so falls are less dangerous? The phrase "We are doing it for your own good" froze most of our hearts when we were children: what does it mean to an adult who has spent anything up to eighty years making his or her own decisions *and* survived? It might be more honest to say "We're doing this because we don't know what else to do!" At least then everyone is feeling impotent together.

b)   We protect older people from their families, particularly if the older person is 'our client'. It is all too easy to act as a go-between with clients and their families, to justify an older person's behaviour, and be critical of family members who do not give whole-hearted support. We might be shocked at Mrs. Peebles not being able to see her sister, but be quite ready to prevent a confrontation between an elderly client and his or her family. Yet such protection is an attempt to prevent the older person from being a part of that which goes on. It might also be a denial of history. Struggles and crises in families with an older member are likely to be action replays of earlier conflicts. They may be heightened or intensified by the effects of old age, but they are part of each family's life. Such crises cannot be dealt with satisfactorily by attempting to protect one of the key members from the heat of the fight.

c)   We protect older people from neighbours, and this is not uncommonly the cause of admission to residential care. Mrs. Peebles stayed in the community until her death despite a great deal of disquiet from neighbours. To begin with when her neighbours demanded that something be done, we would tell them that we were doing all we could and not to worry. Later demands were met with statements about freedom of choice and the right to live at home. As time went by the pressure from neighbours increased as did our attempts to rebuff them. But alongside this went a decline in our confidence that we could continue to protect our client from this pressure .

Had we persisted in our response to the neighbours, I have little doubt that Mrs. Peebles would have been persuaded to agree to leave her home. As it was we decided to withdraw our protection and in response to a particularly worrying incident called a meeting with the neighbours at Mrs. Peebles' flat. Mrs. Peebles met her critics and they met her. The upshot of this meeting (which itself seemed something of an anti-climax) was that Mrs. Peebles' behaviour changed dramatically and the neighbours became tolerant. In subsequent years meetings between Mrs. Peebles and her neighbours were a routine response to crises and she was allowed to remain in the community. Our protection had not been necessary.

The fact is that protection is not only unnecessary, it is usually harmful. The following story illustrates how protectiveness undermines even the best work.

Sisters, Sons and Mothers

I am struck by the number of sisters turning up in this book yet I can think of no instance of brothers. That sisterly relationships feature so importantly in old age might suggest that we should take them more seriously when working with younger age groups.

In this instance, the sisters were Miss Penfold and Mrs. Green. The family tree over shows the key figures

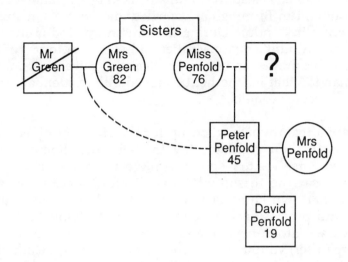

Miss Penfold and Mrs. Green were both clients of the Home Care Team, but Mrs. Green was her sister's main carer. This had been the case for as long as we had known them. They lived on the same balcony in a block of council flats and though Miss Penfold slept in her own flat, she spent the days with Mrs. Green. Miss Penfold's grandson David also spent several nights a week at his grandmother's flat while he was studying in London. Miss Penfold did almost nothing for herself. The home help thought she was probably capable of more but had somehow managed to persuade her family to do things for her. As Mrs. Green grew more frail, more services were provided and the home help and a local volunteer visited daily.

It was Mrs. Green who died first. Who was to look after Miss Penfold? The home care team had a policy of supporting anyone wanting to stay in his or her own home whatever the degree of physical or mental impairment, and Miss Penfold was quite clear she wanted to stay where she was. We geared the service up to this while the family gathered for Mrs. Green's funeral. It was at this time that we began to collect more information. There had always been 'something wrong' with Miss Penfold and she had always needed looking after. She had disgraced the family by having an 'illegitimate' child and then left the child for her sister to care for. Peter Penfold was brought up by his aunt, while his mother remained a shadowy figure disliked by the family. He was an accountant in Birmingham, married and with a son studying engineering in London. During the stressful period immediately following his aunt's death Mr. Penfold was seen to be rude and unkind to his mother and openly critical of her every action. When he demanded that his mother be moved into residential care, the scene was set for conflict.

We were a team which stood up for the rights of older people, particularly their right to stay in their own home. We had organised ourselves to respond with great speed to crises such as these and saw no reason why Miss Penfold should not remain living in her own home. A few days after the funeral we held a family and professionals meeting at Miss Penfold's flat. Present were Miss Penfold, her son and grandson, home help and home help organiser, volunteer and volunteer organiser, health visitor, social worker and me. I was the only person not well known to Miss Penfold, who spent most of the meeting muttering to herself and occasionally swearing at us.

Mr. Penfold said his piece and with such vehement bitterness towards his mother, the whole room was soon against him – except his son who managed to hold a neutral position from which he supported any constructive statement. This young man's central part in the subsequent affairs of the family was both recognised and missed at this meeting. It was clear that he had made much of his grandmother's flat his own and as he spent weekdays in London, he would remain a significant person in her life. But we missed his greater significance. Seeing everyone's anger towards Mr. Penfold for his unsympathetic attitude, it was not difficult to persuade the whole professional network to commit themselves to the community care of Miss Penfold. Her son had no choice but to accept this position, but he did so reluctantly and refused to give his support. This was not a happy way to begin a long and arduous task and within a few weeks, the volunteer, who was also a neighbour, found the family-professionals conflict too onerous and withdrew. Home help time was increased, creating pressure elsewhere in the service.

For several months this went on more or less successfully. We had decided to minimise any responsibility David might feel for his grandmother's care, since supporting us would put him in a conflict of loyalty with his father. However, there came a week when both Miss Penfold's home helps were absent from work. We knew she was distressed by new people and so accepted David's offer to keep an eye on her for us. The offer was genuine but it was also natural, when his grandmother behaved bizarrely one night, for David to call his father, who in turn called an ambulance and drove immediately to London himself. Within a few days Miss Penfold, incomprehensible and incontinent, was transferred to a long stay geriatric ward where some months later she died. It was a salutary lesson in the power and influence of families. In their twenty four hour a day, seven-days-a-week involvement, families offer a degree of commitment that no professional service can ever quite match. So to act against families, without serious efforts to act *with* them, is usually a recipe for failure.

In this case, our determination to protect Miss Penfold from her family had led us to ignore three vital aspects of this three-generational family's situation. Firstly, we did not acknowledge the importance of Mr. Penfold's own bereavement. We recognised his mother's loss but not her son's. Mr. Penfold had, in fact, been more of a son to his aunt and she more of a mother, so he had in effect lost a mother. In our conflict with him and from our position as Miss Penfold's protectors we could not see Mr. Penfold's own pain and so did not respond to it. Had there been any possibility of rapprochement it was lost when we chose to isolate him. The second factor was also obvious but ignored. Mr. Penfold had lost his 'good' mother and was left with his 'bad' mother to remind him of the world's unfairness. The depth of his feeling towards Miss Penfold was a measure of his sense of abandonment by her. That everyone was *still* looking after her when she had not looked after him was hard to take at a time when bereavement had once again left him vulnerable. If we had been able to acknowledge, even if not support, the family's different sense of justice, we might have been able to reach a compromise.

And finally David's part. Mr. Penfold had struggled hard to make his way in the world and if he was determined about anything, it was that his son would receive a better start. David's living arrangements, though a little unusual, represented security for him during his studies. This was of crucial importance to his father and Mrs. Green's death had upset the delicate balance. Mr. Penfold's vehemence towards his mother was, therefore, driven as much by concern for his son as by his own feelings of anger and loss. Again, had we recognised this as part of David's significance we may have been able to converse with Mr. Penfold rather than enter battle with him.

As it was, our urge to protect Miss Penfold from the wrath of her son led to her death in the dismal surroundings of a geriatric back-ward. In thinking how we might have done this differently, I have wondered what difference it would have made if Miss Penfold had not been elderly. I am sure we would have given her much more *conditional* sympathy and would probably have found much more reason to feel sympathy for her son. If we had been acting more professionally, we would have stepped back from taking sides while at the same time tuning in to both points of view; we would have tried to help the pair resolve their conflicts without becoming a party to them ourselves. Ultimately we would have regarded them as two adults with a long history and well able to take responsibility for the eventual outcome of the conflict. Whether the outcome happened to meet with *our* approval or not was immaterial – it was a decision the family had the right to arrive at itself.

So why did we treat Miss Penfold as though she did not share responsibility for the relationship with her son? Why didn't we leave them to it? Of course, we couldn't. We had a statutory responsibility to provide services and, indeed, the son was demanding we do just that (though he was asking for a different service). It is only natural that when we have such a major contribution to make to a family's circumstances, we also want to take some control. Our legitimate control, however, is only over the services we dispense; we have no right to use this power to attempt to exert control over others. We may attempt to do so for the very best of intentions but, once again, it is these very intentions that can lead to someone else's hell.

Empowering older people

Protection is contrary to most older people's interests because it belittles or disempowers them – it contains 'the message' you are no longer able to look after 'yourself'. If the world treats you as incapable of looking after yourself you are likely to lose the opportunities to do so. Deprived of the means to share, participate and control, you will not be able to look after yourself and the world will be proved right. This is the essential bind for older people living in an ageist world.

It is here that systems theory, so useful in declaring an inviolable place in the world for older people, falls down. A central tenet of systems theory, the theory which underlines family therapy, is that systems are made up of interacting parts and that no single part can have more or less influence on the whole than any other single part. Unfortunately, the real world is not as fair as the world described by theory, and we know full well that some people have more power and influence than others. It is this fact, together with the fact that some people abuse their power, which drives us towards protecting older people, for older people make up one of the largest and most discriminated against minorities in our society. Discrimination on the grounds of old age is built in to almost every facet of our lives: economic, social and medical segregation are part of our normal expectations for the treatment of older people, and few of us relish being there ourselves. We treat older people as less than whole, less than fully capable, less than responsible. Terms like 'the elderly' (which is not even a noun) lump several million individual people into one bundle of stereotypes; 'little' and 'dear old ladies' are all that is recognised of women with a lifetime of experience, struggle and achievement; men are reduced to 'old gentlemen' (and then sometimes live up to the part by smelling like public lavatories); and hospital patients become 'geriatrics', which I understand to be a branch of medicine. But one of the worst insults must be attributed to an unnamed family therapist. There is very little literature on family therapy and older people, and seeing a reference to a paper in a British journal, I was eager to read it. The first sentence referred to the management of 'dements' and the article went on to display a total lack of humanity towards the author's clients – it could well have been an article about dying but much loved dogs.

Such an approach is not universal, but it is not uncommon. I know of two occupational therapists who, as part of their induction on joining a team, spent a day at an old people's home. They arrived at seven in the morning to experience 'getting up' time. They found three domestic staff struggling to ensure sixty people were washed, dressed and seated at their places by eight o'clock. These staff were among the lowest paid council employees; they worked nights to support young families, two of them having social security as the only alternative. Their clients had to be ready for breakfast before they could leave one to another job, another to take her children to school. Caught in a trap of their own, their answer was to debase their clients and in the process themselves. Old people queued to be strip-washed by women with thick rubber gloves and old rags. Sometimes doors were ajar, men able to see their female breakfast companions naked. Those not fast enough to dress themselves were thrust into skirts and cardigans, not always their own, and then hustled and bustled to the dining room, where it was hoped they would sit at the same place they always sat because each person's medication was already laid out on their plates. Neither of the occupational therapists slept well that night and both were still distressed at work the next day. A carefully worded factual report was sent through the various bureaucratic channels and in the meetings, arguments, justifications and recriminations that followed the most constant and concrete criticism was against the occupational therapists for *writing* the report instead of "discussing it with those concerned". It was years later that an external inspection, triggered by another more public event, found these practices and more to be routine in this and several other homes.

In one way hearing this story was a boost to the fortunes of the Home Care Team. We had struggled to maintain our view that no person should need to leave his or her own home unless he or she was positively wishing this. Many of our colleagues thought such a position was too extreme and that once people were persuaded to leave their homes, especially those homes which were dirty and smelt, they would realise they were better off in care. We now had proof that whatever conditions were like in an older person's own home, they could well be worse in care. After this we were able to introduce a procedure in which no person was admitted to an old people's home without an assessment and approval by the Home Care Team. Except for those staff committed to 'knowing best' and finding ways round the system, only two people moved into care over the next three years. Both positively demanded it.

It was the Home Care Team's occupational therapist who most helped us to think about empowering older people while recognising their limitations and vulnerabilities.

They defined their task as helping people with disabilities achieve the maximum possible independence. They saw this as a client's right but, more interestingly, they also saw it as a client's responsibility – so they made demands on them! And this is what the team learned to do. Being a 'whole' person does not mean having two functioning arms, legs and whatever else, it means using the abilities one has to the full. In this sense we are all less than whole but no more whole than the frailest most disabled older person. The nuns at my infant school used to say that when you get to heaven, whether you are a bucket, a cup or a thimble, you will be full to the brim with happiness! Wholeness is making the most of what you've got.

Empowerment is enabling a person to make the most of what he or she has. Agnes was empowered by the belief that her relationship with her sister would be more likely to survive continued honesty than a departure into deceit. Miss Peebles was empowered when we found a way for her to use once again her ability to communicate clearly with the world. Miss Penfold may have been empowered with assistance from us to sit face to face with her son and for them both to hear each other.

Empowerment may also mean erring on the side of apparent harshness. When assessing a person's physical or mental ability, it is always easier (and usually safer) to be conservative – to assume they can do less rather than more. But when the tendency is to err on the side of more competence than the assessment suggests, greater demands are made on the client. One of my earliest lessons in family therapy was that to make demands of a family, provided they appeared to be within the family's ability, was the single most effective intervention in the therapy. And it is true that we often achieve things not because we believe it possible ourselves but because someone else important believes it first. Being 'uncaring' and 'unresponsive' to older people is certainly not in their interests, but it may often be less damaging than being too caring and too protective.

There will always be a struggle between too much and too little care for older people; between seeing their strengths and seeing their weaknesses. For the foreseeable future this struggle will be conducted in a social environment essentially hostile to older people – and this is an environment to which they and we have contributed. At the sharpest end of the task of caring for older people, the home helps, residential staff, nurses and families themselves have little hope of always getting it right – too few resources, personal or otherwise, will often work against the person with least power and least say. But most people in this position do anything but give up.

The following chapters are accounts of how families, professionals and older people themselves have collaborated, struggled and sometimes fought to do anything but give up.

CHAPTER 3

WALKER'S LAST STAND

THE INTERACTIONAL VIEW

One of the difficulties which for many years dogged family therapists was our belief that we needed to see families. This was a double difficulty because it precluded not only all those families who didn't want to be seen, but also all those potential clients who had no families. Working in a team with one thousand elderly clients, the majority of whom were on their own, presented quite a challenge, especially as the team's most difficult-to-solve problems were by and large associated with very isolated older people with no family at all. If family therapy was to survive it would have to transcend the need for families. And it did. Family therapy is a treatment method only in its narrowest sense. Considered more broadly, it is a way of looking at the world.

The interactional view offers an alternative of looking at mental and psychological health. We can all be driven mad given a sufficiently malign and distorted environment, and some of us will go mad quicker than others. Whatever our natural propensity for sanity is will determine how much pressure or stress we can take, but the deciding factor on the question of mental health is more likely to be what happens between the individual and his or her environment rather than what happens within the individual's own psyche.

In psychological matters the significant environment is other people and for most of us the most significant other people are our families. Family therapy therefore grew out of an understanding of personal problems generated by, and therefore solvable by, the network of close relationships of which each individual is a part. For most of this century we have attempted to understand people and what they do by looking inside them, whether it be inside their bodies or their 'psyches'. Real medicine is seen to be anything which adjusts the body with surgery, chemicals, radiation or whatever, and real 'mind' treatment is expected to be lengthy, in depth exploration of individual experience. A much more telling reality is, however, the relationship between health and environment. Stress-related illnesses and those associated with unhealthy food or pollution probably account for more poor health in Britain than all the other causes put together. The impact of environment on health at a world-wide level is even more striking. A society's overall health is not so much a product of medicine, but a product of the environment and an individual's relationship with that environment.

One of the earliest influences on the development of family therapy, and the most lasting, was that of Gregory Bateson[2]. Bateson was among other things an anthropologist and worked with his wife Margaret Mead. In the 1950's his interest began to focus on communication, firstly at a tribal level and later at the family level. It was his study of the communication patterns in families of schizophrenic patients which led him directly to family therapy. Bateson and his colleagues identified incongruent communications as a potentially causal factor in schizophrenia. In particular they developed the 'double bind' theory to describe how a person subjected to conflicting demands over a long period of time, and unable to escape the conflict, will in effect be 'split in two'. The Bateson research isolated such factors as the spoken word and the tone of voice and body language making it possible for one person to give a double message: for example, asking for love with words and rejecting it with body language. With this theory the 'cause' of schizophrenia was taken out of the individual and placed within the relationships the individual has with significant others. The move was made from an individualistic view to an interactional view – no longer what happens *within*, but, instead, what happens *between*.

Unfortunately, not only was this one of the sources of family therapy, it was also the start of one of family therapy's greatest problems. R.D. Laing, Bateson's most successful populariser, took the theory to its more obvious and most immediate conclusion:

---

2 Bateson G. "Steps to an Ecology of the Mind" *Ballentine Books* (1972) A Collection of Bateson's most important papers some of which are heavy going!

parents, mothers especially, are the cause of schizophrenia – and, indeed, most 'individual' problems. Ever since the charge that family therapists blame families has stuck and as a result, clients and professionals have treated it with suspicion. This is unfortunate, if not always unjustified, because Bateson's thesis, as he himself would have been the first to say, was only half way there. In a purely interactional world everything causes everything else – it can be as equally argued and as equally true that a family's behaviour is a response to the schizophrenic member's behaviour as much as the schizophrenic person is responding to the family. It is a part of our culture that we want to find the cause of things and where possible allocate responsibility and even blame. But it does get in the way of problem *solving*. For me the interactional view is not so much of interest as an explanation of how problems occur, but more as a way of bringing to bear on the problem *influences* which can lead to change. If we are affected by what goes on around us, then altering what goes on around a person with a problem will affect that person and maybe affect the problem. If we can understand the problem as being, in part, a result of interactional patterns – the relationships between the person with the problem and his or her significant others – then an adjustment to those patterns is likely to have a direct bearing on the problem.

An interactional approach to problem-solving is not, therefore, confined to problem-solving within families. It has become associated with families because that is for most of us our closest set of relationships, but it holds for all relationships, including those between clients and professionals and even relationships between professionals themselves.

One of the great advantages of the interactional view is its applicability over the whole range of welfare services – it is not just an approach to counselling. For most people working with older clients this is of enormous importance. Few services to older people are within the realm of therapy or counselling. Most are administered by home care teams, meals on wheels organisations, day centres, residential homes, community nurses and hospitals. They include housework, bath seats, meals, transport, ulcer dressing, incontinence supplies, social activities, outings and home visiting. All of these services can be and often are 'therapeutic' in their effect. Delivered in a caring and sensitive manner to those who need them, they enhance rather than diminish a person's independence and autonomy. But what happens when a person who needs them refuses such services, or receives them without gaining more independence in the process? What happens when a client constantly complains or is always depressed, or behaves abusively to those providing a service? Such clients might well benefit from counselling but rarely would they see this themselves. In these circumstances, theories about the individual are not very helpful – the individual is not accessible to the approach these theories require. With an interactional view, however, it is perfectly possible to view the client's behaviour as connected to the professional's behaviour and vice versa – this is not saying the professionals cause the behaviour, just that each is part of the other's environment and so is affecting the other's behaviour. It is, therefore, possible to change the client's behaviour by changing that of the professionals. The following is a case in point.

THE STORY OF MR. WALKER

The Referral

Mr. Walker was a tramp whose itinerant life had radiated from Camden Town in north London. As his legs became weaker, the length of his journeys shortened until in his late sixties (as far as anyone knew) he could tramp no more. He found a home in the garden shed of a large house near Camden Town and a generous owner allowed him to stay there. Mr. Walker kept himself to himself and, legs and weather permitting, took short walks in the neighbourhood. All went well until Mr. Walker's benefactor decided to move and needed to sell house and shed with vacant possession. As a 'vulnerable' person under housing legislation, Mr. Walker was rehoused in a council owned bed-sit, part of an old house converted to rehouse single men from a nearby hostel which was being closed.

In the run-up to the move Mr. Walker's health suffered and he was referred by a housing officer to the home care team. At this time he was also found to be suffering from diabetes. Mr. Walker was not a communicative man, but he said yes to the services offered and once he had moved, began receiving meals on wheels, daily insulin injections and a twice-weekly home help. From the start Mr. Walker generated neither respect nor warmth. When he spoke at all to his visitors he spoke abusively and never once did he show appreciation of the help he was being given. He was seen to be a 'difficult' client and on top of this was not liked. It is often the case with clients who are difficult to please that those caring for them fall out with each other. This certainly happened between the home help and the visiting nurses, neither side being convinced that the other was pulling their weight. Things went on like this for some months, the situation remaining far from ideal but always manageable: until Mr. Walker started becoming violent. The nurses began visiting in pairs, which seemed to incense Mr. Walker further, and when he caught one of them a blow with his stick, they decided, quite legitimately, that this was well beyond the call of duty. The service was withdrawn.

The Problem

As if exhausted by this onslaught, Mr. Walker took to his bed. The home help found him there the next day and judged by the state of his sheets and blankets that he had not moved. All attempts the home help made to clean him up were angrily repelled and the home help was asked to return the next day. This she did; Mr. Walker had still not moved but he was as strongly abusive as ever, wielding his stick each time the home help approached. By the third day Mr. Walker and his bed were awash with bodily waste but he was as adamant as ever in his refusal of help. On the fourth day the home help organiser went to see Mr. Walker and found him in a coma. She called an ambulance. One of the crew must have been new and stood outside vomiting as the home help organiser and remaining crew person carried Mr. Walker, wrapped in black bin-bags, to the ambulance. His flat was cleaned up and four days later he was discharged from hospital in good health. Mr. Walker went straight to his bed and refused to move.

The Dilemma

The home help organiser called an emergency meeting of the team to consider what to do about Mr. Walker. It was this same home help organiser who had precipitated the team into its decision to remove no one from their own home unless he or she positively wished to move. At a team meeting a year or two earlier she had rather tentatively admitted that in fifteen years as a home help and then home help organiser, she had never met anyone for whom a forced or even persuaded move could be justified. She had seen many such moves take place and had even assumed they must be right, since more qualified people than her were behind them. Nevertheless, she herself had never been able to understand why and had always felt a sense of unease about her acceptance of this all-too-standard practice. It then turned out that none of the eight member team with over fifty years of experience in front line work with older people – could remember a case of justifiable removal or persuasion. From that day on the team undertook to do all it could to respect each client's right to choose.

The home help organiser began the 'Mr. Walker' meeting by reminding the team of her earlier statement: "I know it was me who said we should never remove anyone from their own home against their wishes and I still believe that we shouldn't, but at the same time if we don't move Mr. Walker I think he will die and I will have his death on my conscience for the rest of my life and I couldn't live with that." She had stated the dilemma that every professional who works with older people faces time and time again, and the team did their best to avoid it. We blamed the nurses, the housing department, the referrer, the owner of the shed, the hospital and whoever else we could think of; we "if only'd" about other sheds, about our earlier treatment of Mr. Walker, about hospitals with more beds than patients but when we came down to it, we could not really say any of our colleagues had done any less than their best. And Mr. Walker still lay there, a few hundred yards away, presenting his dilemma.

It is in situations such as this that Bateson's ideas about communication and the interactional approach to therapy which his colleagues subsequently developed prove most useful. The home help organiser had stated what appeared to be a 'no win' situation – giving up her principals or risking Mr. Walker's life. It is not uncommon for families, individuals or organisations to present problems in terms of dilemmas in which whatever choice is made, it is the wrong one. Though they may not in this form lead to schizophrenia, they almost invariably lead to stress. However, viewed as *part* of an interaction they can frequently be resolved. Dilemmas or binds in one part of an interactional system must be mirrored in other parts. If the home help organiser was in a bind, then so was her client. In Mr. Walker's case he was saying loudly and clearly *leave me alone*, but was their another message?

If someone really wants to be left alone to die, do they do it in such a "noisy" way? And if that was what Mr. Walker really wanted, didn't he know every quiet corner in North London where he could do just that? Mr. Walker was giving a double message and we gave a double message back.

The Work

After the team meeting the home help organiser went round to Mr. Walker's and said: "Mr. Walker, I've thought a lot about you and I've listened to what you've said. You know that I don't agree with what you are doing and that I think you would be better off allowing us to help you – because that is what we want to do – help you. But I have listened to you and because I respect you, I will accept your wishes. But I want to ask you for something in return. I hope for my sake you will agree to this. If I stop helping you, I am worried that you will die and I will then have your death on my conscience for the rest of my life. I would like you to agree to let me call round for a few minutes every other day, just so I can reassure myself that you are still alive. I promise faithfully that I will not help you on these visits." Mr. Walker reluctantly agreed and asked the home help organiser to pass his cigarettes before she left. She refused, as this would be a breach of promise. She then endured ten minutes of abuse and left. She returned two days later to an almost exact repeat, and so began one of the most difficult two weeks of her career. Each visit lasted ten minutes, sitting just out of range of Mr. Walker's stick. He lay in bed getting filthier and filthier and more and more ill-looking. Each time he asked for something, he was reminded of the promise and this would precipitate him into another barrage of foul abuse. The home help organiser agonised after each visit, particularly as time went by, but with the team's support she kept her strength. Mr. Walker, too, had hidden resources – he always had cigarettes and fresh milk in his room, where from she never knew or asked. To keep her promise the home help organiser visited on Good Friday and Easter Sunday, and on some days it was touch and go whether or not she called an ambulance.

The Care

A constant problem in the delivery of community service is how to care by not caring. Situations like that of Mr. Walker invariably divide professionals into those who think his wish to be left alone should be respected and those who think his survival needs should be met come what may. While most people would subscribe to the first position in theory, they will in practice follow the more pragmatic path of keeping their client alive. The problem with the first path, at its face value at least, is the client's view of the behaviour of professionals. If the caring decision is to respect the client's wish to be left alone, how does the client distinguish between this and abandonment? How does he or she know that the absence is filled with respect, concern and even anxiety. For many clients the answer is that they won't unless the non-provision of services is somehow made concrete. This was why only the home help organiser could visit Mr. Walker in this way. Had the more obvious choice of a social worker been made, this would not have been a 'non-service' it would have been yet another service for Mr. Walker to fight against. But as the home help organiser's role was to provide a particular service – that of a home help – her visits and refusals to 'help' were proof of her continued and caring involvement, despite the withdrawal of service.

The End

Then one day Mr. Walker was up and surveying his mess. He said he thought he would have someone to help him clean up – occasionally. So he had a home help, but no nurse and no meals-on-wheels. Throughout his life Mr. Walker had shunned society and continued to do so. He had defined the services he needed as synonymous with loss of freedom and could see no way out of this dilemma. The home help organiser had challenged this definition, not by words which would have sounded empty, but by an action which resolved both her dilemma and his – she needed neither force him to leave, nor let him die; and he learned that this particular service, at least, did not represent a significant loss of freedom.

SUMMARY

The interactional view is interested in the invisible lines of relationship with which we are connected to one another. Relationships are immensely complex and can be made up of many different layers. Some aspects of a single relationship between two people may quite easily be in conflict and where these conflicting aspects are equally important, relationship problems are likely to develop. Mr. Walker's behaviour can be seen in terms of such a dilemma. He wanted the freedom to remain socially isolated but required a degree of contact as an 'insurance policy' against further deterioration of health. Caught with conflicting needs, he made conflicting demands: leave me but don't leave me. Understood in this way it was possible, given the commitment and professionalism of the home help organiser, to meet both aspects of Mr. Walker's request – to leave him without help but not without connection. As he experienced both requests being met, Mr. Walker's dilemma dissolved and he was able to accept a service both for its own value and as a symbol of a more generalised care. Mr. Walker continued to live in this way for a number of years.

than most of us, and to protect them from everyday conflict is little short of insulting. We all know good relationships don't exist without a degree of conflict, and if we are to use our relationships with clients to their full value, we must be prepared to fight as well as love. Being professional does not exempt us from human feelings and frailties. It is probably safer to assume that a good proportion of our clients, by virtue of what they have survived and achieved are actually stronger than we are and that sometimes our wish to avoid conflict with them is not so much to protect them, as to protect ourselves.

THE STORY OF MISS KELLEHER

Miss Kelleher was in her eighties when the arthritis she suffered from took a turn for the worse and she began experiencing great pain just lifting a knife and fork. Like Miss Proudfoot she had led an independent life and held a job of considerable importance during the Second World War. She was in warden-supervised housing and her rather high-handed approach to professionals had not made her very popular. She was also strong willed and the warden wisely kept out of her way as much as possible. She had a home help visiting every day to prepare her breakfast, and an occupational therapist was called to reassess her needs. There was a variety of equipment which could be installed to help Miss Kelleher, but what she really wanted was an automatic feeding device – something like a small, mechanical shovel. The occupational therapist would not agree to this, partly because she knew it to be of limited use and partly because she could teach Miss Kelleher to eat with adapted cutlery. A long battle ensued and I was eventually brought in as the occupational therapist's manager.

By this time the situation had become quite 'stuck', with the home help and occupational therapist falling out, and then two district nurses also falling out with the occupational therapist (the nurses visited to dress Miss Kelleher's ulcers; two had been assigned to counter her 'overbearing' character). Throughout this the occupational therapist was struggling to teach Miss Kelleher new feeding skills, but when she wasn't there, the home help and the nurses had been spoon feeding Miss Kelleher. It was a particularly strong double dose of two-against-one triangles (Miss enough and most older people content themselves with what is available. But this is not always the case. A person might feel alone and uncared for, and for want of anything else, request community services. If the sense of loneliness and need remains, what else is there but to seek more of the only care available? If the need for care is still felt, then even more services might be requested. In each case the services available do not sufficiently reflect the felt need and as the client becomes more desperate, the demand for care, channelled into a request for more services, becomes more insistent. If the service providers lose patience with such a client, then the client can even begin to feel less cared for as services increase. Caught in this vicious cycle, it is quite possible for a client to end up in residential care and still be unhappy and uncared for. Mr. More was a client who nearly went this way.

THE STORY OF MR. MORE

The Referral

A health visitor asked for Mr. More to be urgently assessed for residential care. He was not managing at home and had begun to fall. Mr. More was well known to the home care team, with a home help and volunteer each making twice weekly visits. He was one of the team's more frequent telephone callers, quick to become anxious if his home help was late. Mr. More's wife had died nine years previously and he had no other family. He was not a very sociable person and like most of the team's more worrying clients did not wish to attend a day centre. Mr. More had never been a serious worry to the team and, therefore, the health visitor's request came as something of a surprise.

The Assessment

The team began its assessment by seeking the views of the home help and the volunteer. The result was something of a shock. Instead of visiting twice a week, the volunteer was calling on Mr. More every day except Sunday, and the home help was making two unauthorised visits in his own time. Both had been persuaded of the need by Mr. More and as neither thought the increase would be supported by their superiors, neither reported the extra time being spent. It was obviously a relief to both workers to be able to tell the real story: the volunteer declared a deterioration in his own health and his inability to continue providing such care to Mr. More. He thought he was quite inadequate to Mr. More's needs and suggested we find a younger, more dedicated volunteer to really care for him. The home help was also reluctant to keep visiting Mr. More. He said he found him impossible to satisfy and, in his opinion, Mr. More would always want more however much he was given. Meanwhile, the health visitor was insisting that Mr. More was beyond community care and needed to move into an old people's home.

The next stage of the assessment was for the home help organiser and volunteer organiser to reassess Mr. More's needs for their services if he were to remain at home. One of the team's occupational therapists also undertook a full assessment of Mr. More's functional ability, as well as finding out Mr. More's own wishes with regard to residential care.

The occupational therapist found Mr. More to be fully capable of taking physical care of himself, his flat and his shopping, but acknowledged a psychological need for continued service provision. The home help organiser concurred with this view and could find no justification for increasing Mr. More's allocation of home help time beyond the two days per week previously agreed. Similarly, the volunteer organiser could not justify almost daily visiting to someone quite capable of going out, when she had so many housebound people in more obvious need. The assessment was co-ordinated by the team's social worker: in his view, whatever the 'objective' abilities and needs of Mr. More, something was not being met and unless this changed, the health visitor's continuing prediction would soon be proved accurate.

The Dilemma

One way a client's dilemmas might interact with his or her professional carers is for different aspects of the dilemma to be taken up by different professionals. This appeared to be happening with Mr. More. The volunteer was hearing his call for help, the home help was hearing his exasperation that the help was of the wrong sort and, therefore, never satisfying, and the health visitor was responding to his hopelessness, that it would be best to give up everything. The volunteer and home help organisers, from their slightly more removed positions, saw Mr. More in relation to other clients and deemed his needs to be more psychological than physical opinion which was substantiated by the occupational therapist's assessment. From an even more distant perspective, the social worker knew that somehow these differences needed to be reconciled if Mr. More was going to be helped to remain at home.

The team was caught in another dilemma: if services *were not* increased, it was likely that another crisis would develop and the situation could escalate into one where residential care would be the only option; but if services *were* increased, experience had shown that there would be pressure for even more services leading ultimately to residential care – something Mr. More had always professed not to want. As with Mr. Walker before him, Mr. More and the team appeared to be in a no-win situation.

The Network Meeting

By this time the team had begun to use meetings between clients and their professional networks as the starting point for resolving the more difficult problems. Very often the simple act of meeting and sharing information and opinions would be enough to set in motion a solution to whatever problem had caused the meeting to be called in the first place. In situations like Mr. More's, however, there is a risk that the conflict will be heightened as opposite views are expressed, countered and reasserted. It would do Mr. More no good to have his personal dilemma reflected and acted out before him in a way which tightened rather than loosened its hold on his future. In order for such a meeting to succeed it is necessary for someone, preferably the person chairing the meeting, to realise that everyone is right, that each view must be taken seriously and that the essence of each person's preferred solution is incorporated into the final outcome. It is no easy task to chair a meeting where harsh truths need to be expressed and opposing opinions need equal recognition and validation, while at the same time, treating the client with honesty and respect. The social worker had these skills and each person – health visitor, home help, volunteer, their managers and Mr. More himself were all able to express their views. It is usually the case that when our views are heard, we become more able to hear the views of others. As each professional involved with Mr. More felt their view validated, they were more able to listen to and appreciate the views of the others. For his part Mr. More could experience the sharing of his dilemma in a constructive way, and for the first time it was possible to envisage the reconciliation of these apparently conflicting demands. In order to achieve this reconciliation, Mr. More had to receive less (or at least the original amount of) service and more care; yet, in the long run, the care would have to be a component of the standard service, as no other forms of home care were either available or acceptable.

The earlier success with Mr. Walker had led the team to realise that where a service was somehow seen to be uncaring, it was necessary to alter *action* in order to alter the client's perception. It was not useful just stating that the services are given caringly, some concrete symbol or token of that care has to be demonstrated. This, of course, is true of all relationships: each side has to *give* if the relationship is to continue and each must give *more* if it is to deepen. To convince Mr. More of the care behind the service, the team had to give *more* while not increasing the service. What was required was, therefore, a more personal investment and one over which Mr. More could have some control.

The network meeting with Mr. More reached a critical point when Mr. More, bowing to the professionals opinion of his physical capacity compared with other less able people, acquiesced to a resumption of twice-weekly visiting. This acquiescence could have been taken as agreement, but it was clear that Mr. More was far from satisfied. If the meeting had ended there, it is almost certain that he would have felt so uncared for that his behaviour would reflect this and a crisis would have been precipitated. On the other hand, not to accept it would push the decision in an equally unproductive direction. The social worker, therefore, accepted the offer but with the gravest doubts attached to his acceptance. He was grateful for Mr. More's co-operation in trying to manage with less help, but he was sharply aware that the team's assessment of need was not always accurate and he had doubts that enough service was being provided. To cover this doubt he asked Mr. More to agree to have a condition attached to the agreement. The condition was that every day one of the team would call by to see if he was managing. If at any time Mr. More reported that he was not managing, extra help would be provided immediately. Mr. More brightened visibly and the meeting ended with a sense of the possibility of success. The team were less pleased. A daily visit seemed a most burdensome requirement, until the logic of the decision was clarified.

The Work

The team was already committed, even though unwittingly, to almost daily visits in one form or another. The social worker had thought that for the team to demonstrate absolute good faith, Mr. More had to experience them as offering even more than he had so far received. Though the daily visits would be extremely brief – maybe no more than a minute or two – they indicated that Mr. More was being thought about *every* day, not just for six days. And as no 'service' was being provided, the visits could be seen as being something extra for Mr. More himself, rather than for Mr. More as a service recipient. Finally, the visits had nothing to do with Mr. More's incapacities but rather afforded him an opportunity to demonstrate what he could do. He was at last in a position of strength. He could remain independent yet receive a daily visit, just to 'see how he was', for as long as he wished. The deal struck was that the visits would do exactly that – continue until Mr. More *and* the team were convinced that such concern was no longer necessary.

The End

Six weeks later the team was beginning to regret the price it had paid for the solution to Mr. More's problem. And then one day Mr. More said he had been thinking for some time that the checking up was unnecessary and while they could certainly continue, as far as he was concerned, he now *knew* he could manage.

Mr. More went on to manage with this basic provision for a number of years. The change occurred because the team, by their actions, had changed Mr. More's perception of the services being provided. He had needed to experience *in his own way* the caring quality of these services. Once he had concrete evidence of care (the daily visits), he could accept that it existed without such constant and overt demonstration. What the team went on to find was that investments of time and effort such as these invariably 'paid off' and led to an overall reduction in the efforts needed. A few minutes a day for six weeks was a small price to pay for several years of amicable and trusting relationship.

Postscript: Three years later

Three years later it was my last day with the team (I was about to move to a job in a Child Psychiatry Department!); I was in the home care team room when a home help organiser banged down the phone saying: "Mr. More – complain, complain, complain – will he ever be satisfied?" I was surprised, as I had not known that we were again at odds with Mr. More. I asked if it was the same client (it was), and how long the complaints had been going on? The organiser thought a moment and then realised what he had done.

Once we have a picture of someone, a way of looking at and understanding him or her, it can be very difficult to change it. Even clear evidence that our picture is distorted may still not lead us to make an adjustment. This is one reason why problems recur – a person who is *seen* as problematic is *treated* as problematic and if a person is *treated* as a problem that person is likely to *become* a problem, and so justify the perception. In this way our attitudes towards and treatment of others can *create* problems where no problem previously existed. In the case of the home help organiser and Mr. More, three years of co-operative and satisfying relationship was forgotten because Mr. More rang up with a complaint. He was then treated as a complainer and brushed off. The scene was set for an instant return to the old problem – Mr. More would now feel uncared for, the more so because his trust had been broken. He would, therefore, complain more and so justify the home help organiser's opinion of him. Fortunately, the lapse was momentary and the organiser rang Mr. More straight back offering to visit that afternoon. The organiser could almost hear Mr. More relax as he replied, "Don't bother, I was just in a bit of a panic but it's all right now – I'll ring you on Monday if I need anything."

An interactional view had provided a way of understanding Mr. More's behaviour in terms of a dilemma and then given a framework for constructing a solution which met both ends of the dilemma. It had also shown how redundant interactions – in this case the old pattern of complaint and counter complaint – can be easily activated and how avoidance of a return to old patterns can be achieved by reinforcing the new ones.

CHAPTER 5

THE LONG ROAD TO MARGATE

GENERATIONAL BOUNDARIES

Parents and Children

An important school of family therapy was developed by Salvador Minuchin and colleagues in the 1960's and 70's. Their view was that in order to do their task, families required a hierarchical organisation with clear boundaries around each generation. Any psychological or relationship problem within the family was seen to be a result of a departure from this basic structure. Minuchin worked successfully with some of the poorest families in New York and later with children suffering from extreme forms of anorexia nervosa, asthma and diabetes. His books record some of the most successful therapy ever accomplished. Working as he did with families who might not come back next week or with children who might die tomorrow, Minuchin developed a very immediate form of therapy. It was not good enough to give clients 'something to think about' or even something to *do* between sessions. He wanted to make changes happen *within* each session. If a father was too close to his daughter and not close enough to his wife, Minuchin would want to change that in the session – perhaps by insisting that the parents discuss the problem without allowing the daughter to interrupt. If parents disagreed about how to deal with a child's temper tantrum Minuchin might ask them to generate a tantrum, and then work out a *joint* way of dealing with it. In developing a therapy suitable for extreme circumstances, Minuchin had found it to be effective in all family situations where a problem exists.

My approach to Agnes and Mary was derived from these *structural* family therapy ideas. Agnes and Mary were sisters, yet over the years had gradually evolved something closer to a parent-child relationship. In structural terms they had formed a hierarchy running contrary to their equal positions as adult siblings. They had also become what Minuchin called 'enmeshed'. Neither could do anything without affecting the other and each was *almost* prepared to give up life or sanity to protect the feelings of the other. Supporting and encouraging Mary to state clearly her own position to her sister was a move to create a *difference* in their relationship *during* the session: it required her to treat Agnes as an equal (woman to woman) and also to own a separate opinion and a wish for a separate course of life. Successful as this intervention was in helping Agnes and Mary move into a new and more harmonious stage of their relationship, it still undermined my confidence in the use of such direct interventions. With younger families creating such intensity of feeling can be extremely uncomfortable, but I have never known it to be fatal. I also have to say that I have never known it to be fatal to older people either, but I do not want to risk being the first to make it so.

It was not long after my fright with Mary and Agnes that I met Mrs. Young. She referred her mother Mrs. Overton for residential care. Had I not met Mary and Agnes, I might have done better by Mrs. Young and her mother but as it was I decided to proceed cautiously.

Becoming an Adult

Jay Haley, who has worked closely with Bateson and Minuchin, wrote one of the most influential family therapy books, *Leaving Home*, in which he argues that problems ranging from criminality to psychosis are associated with a failure to 'leave home'. For white, middle-class westerners, leaving home symbolises the separation of one generation from another and it is this which Haley marks out as the most fundamental life- cycle transition in any culture. Drugs, crime and insanity all provide ways to remain dependent, if not on family then on institutions. Haley's work was with adolescents and young adults, but the effects of failing to establish independence can be seen throughout life.

When a young couple marry they need to adjust to each other and, in doing so, have each to relinquish some of the beliefs and ways of doing things of their own families. Families differ in their flexibility and flexibility is always vulnerable to stress. For some young people there may be quite a struggle to achieve their families' acceptance of their independence and different code of living. This struggle, which to an extent exists for all of us throughout our lives, is not always won. Instead of a woman gaining a husband, her mother gains a son and the new couple remain 'junior' to the older generation. Or the would-be wife finds herself in competition with her husband's mother, who continues to take first place. Subsuming a new spouse into an equally dependent state as his or her partner, subjecting him or her to constant competition from a parent or simply choosing a partner who only wants a 'limited engagement' are all ways of maintaining loyalty to and dependence on parents, while going through the motions of separation and independence.

Staying an Adult

In a gathering of any three people it is rare that one does not feel at least a degree of this dependency – the pull to behave like an adolescent after only two or three hours with a parent. Who knows at what point this pull becomes overpowering. For my part my mother had to be dying before I began to think I was strong enough to stand my ground as an adult. But if I had not been so strong and had to care for her within my own family, I do not know if we would have managed to hold the family together. I once said this in a talk to an Age Concern meeting. Many of the audience were elderly and had looked after parents, spouses and siblings. One man bravely stood up and said that I should not have been invited to speak if I was not prepared to look after my mother (she was in fact quite fit and well at that time – my doubts had been hypothetical). There was a shocked silence after this statement and I felt like disappearing into the floor. Then a middle-aged woman stood up and said with tears in her voice that my statement was the most important thing anyone had ever said and that if she had her time over again she would have said the same. Woman after woman stood to make similar statements – some wishing they had said 'no', some just glad that their burden was recognised at last as more than hard work, and some feeling vindicated that they had not agreed to take an elderly parent into their homes. The painfulness of these spontaneous declarations was almost overwhelming, and the complexity of each person's story makes any summary (including this one) of the intergenerational issues involved, only the crudest shadow.

Just as sisterly relationships have a special richness over time, so too do those between mothers and daughters. In fact, Haley's book was criticised for not acknowledging this special relationship, in which a dependency relationship transforms with adulthood into one equally close but encompassing mutual respect for each other's integrity and difference. However, a relationship with a potential for such positive strength can be just as binding in a negative way – a way which limits growth and independence. When this happens, the implications for family life can be disastrous. Mrs. Young and Mrs. Overton had just such a relationship but before beginning their sad story, the role of carers needs to be acknowledged.

FAMILY CARERS

The man who wanted me to leave the Age Concern meeting had cared for his sick wife for ten years. She had suffered from Alzheimer's disease and until her last few months had lived at home with her husband. He was eighty-two when she died and in the preceding months had helped the hospital speech therapist re-teach language to a woman who had had a brain tumour removed. She was eighty-five and they had married shortly before the conference. The majority of carers, though, are women and often who feel they have little choice. Brought up into the roles of home-maker, physical and emotional care-giver, sometimes at home with children anyway and usually subject to criticism and guilt for not extending this roles to any family member in need, women have a poor chance of standing up for their right to care first for themselves. Neither is it only their own parents they come to care for, it is just as likely to be those of their partner. For many women this is not just a raw deal – it can be a loss of every chance to lead an independent existence – as the woman at the conference said, it can be like a life sentence.

What makes it so is not just the quantity of work, though with a very dependent person this can be enough. It is rather the emotional or relational aspects of the situation. Most relationships come under strain when a situation is difficult. No couple lives without conflict just as no parent-child relationship is without conflict. Under pressure these conflicts can be revived and exacerbated, and it is easy to see how simultaneous intergenerational and couple conflicts can magnify and feed off each other. If one has had a difficult relationship with a parent throughout life, it does not go away with the parent's advancing years; it only goes away if it is resolved. If more counselling were available (and acceptable) to families having to readjust to the growing dependence of an older member, then a great deal fewer sacrifices and tragic endings would result. For Mrs. Overton the counselling came too late.

MRS. OVERTON AND MRS. YOUNG

The Referral

In response to Mrs. Young's referral of her mother, I arranged to visit at a time when all the family would be together. I arrived to find only Mrs. Young. She wanted to speak to me privately. I might have insisted on seeing everyone but I might also have been a little relieved that no great confrontation was going to take place. In any case, Mrs. Young had a right to a consideration of her request on her own terms and this is what she was given.

Mrs. Young was due to be fifty in a few months. In her words she had 'never had a life', and owed one to herself before it was too late. She was married with a fourteen-year-old daughter. Her husband's mother lived nearby and because she was old and frail, he visited her every day and provided much of her care. Mr. and Mrs. Young lived in Mrs. Overton's flat and had always done so since they were married. It began as a temporary convenience and just "went on". Mrs. Overton had not always been well and had spent some time in a psychiatric hospital. For a number of years she had been confused and senile dementia had been diagnosed. Mrs. Young said she had always had to look after her mother and now the burden was intolerable. She was clearly distressed throughout the meeting and her fears for her own mental health did not seem ill founded. We talked about Mrs. Overton's wishes. Her daughter thought she would not understand but would want to stay where she was. My suggestion to Mrs. Young that she might straightforwardly tell her mother she was not going to look after her filled Mrs. Young with horror. She did not imagine she could do it. She wanted me to tell Mrs. Overton she needed a holiday and to move her to a home on that basis. I explained that it would need to be all above-board and left Mrs. Young thinking over the possibility of her telling her mother herself. I arranged to visit again with Mrs. Young, agreeing to have the family there next time.

A Second Referral

Between visits Margaret, Mrs. Young's daughter, was referred for not attending school (I was in a generic social work team at the time!). Not long before I had attended a series of seminars run by Robin Skynner, one of the first and most influential British family therapists, in which he had identified a certain type of non-attendance (where the child stays at home) as evidence of separation difficulties between parent and child. Addressing this issue had proved enormously successful in reducing what he called "school phobia". Later Haley was to identify this and similar problems as one of the warning signs of an inability to move from the childhood to the adult generation and so achieve independence.

The picture this gave of the family was one of a mother–daughter relationship never quite shifting into an adult mode. A partial separation had been achieved through marriage and parenthood, but the marriage had been to someone in a similar position. The marriage 'contract' enabled both partners to remain the daughter and son of their respective mothers, that is to keep their own needs and wishes subservient to those of their parents. Unable to act with full independence as adults, they were unable to lead their daughter to independence. She was being 'groomed' for the next generation of mother-daughter dependency.

Bringing the Generations Together

It was my view then, and to a large extent it still is, that this task of separation has to be done by the "joined-together" people themselves. The removal of one party by an outsider might effect a physical separation but it is likely at the same time to tighten the emotional entanglement. Mrs. Young's hope that I would spirit away her mother was therefore ill-founded – it would not make her any more independent and, if she was to lead something of the life she had missed, she would certainly need to be able to act independently.

Thinking in terms of the family system, two things would help Mrs. Young. Firstly, getting her daughter back to school would make her feel more competent as a parent and therefore more successful as an adult (it would also considerably reduce her worries); and, secondly, encouraging a closer relationship with her husband would again enhance the adult side of her life while giving her support to stand up a little more firmly to the demands of her mother.

The next meeting was attended by the three generations of women but not by Mr. Young. We looked at how Mr. and Mrs. Young could get Margaret off to school (this proved to be successful and Margaret completed her education without further non-attendance). When it came to considering Mrs. Overton's position, Mrs. Young complained in a very apologetic way about her mother. Margaret complained in a more direct way, but in *defence* of her mother, not on her own behalf. Mrs. Overton herself did not appear to be getting a hearing. Here I made a big and very common mistake: I took over the conversation with the older person instead of enabling it to take place between those who *needed* it, Mrs. Overton and her daughter. Of course, Mrs. Overton was no more prepared to talk to me than she was to her daughter and so her silence appeared to confirm her daughter's opinion. In all likelihood, Mrs. Overton was deeply suspicious of me, knew I might be trying to evict her and was frightened. In these circumstances it would not have been wise to give away information even if she could. So we ended with me feeling almost as big a failure as Mrs. Young but with a further card to play – Mr. Young had still kept out. Once again I reiterated the importance of seeing Mr. Young and a new meeting time was fixed.

The Network Meeting

We have already seen with the Penfold family how a hospital admission can provide a 'back door' to care. When a family or a group of professionals are under stress in respect of an older person, that person becomes vulnerable to removal on health grounds. This was what happened with Mrs. Overton, who had a chronic chest complaint and prior to (? because of) my planned visit was admitted to hospital. I first knew of it when the hospital social worker telephoned me to ask who was going to do the residential care application, she or I! I went for one last go. I spoke to Mrs. Young and asked if she would agree to a meeting at the hospital so she could tell her mother herself that she was not going to take her home. It was when I said, "Will you do it if your husband stands by you?" that she agreed. I then phoned Mr. Young and impressed on him the importance of a husband supporting a wife in these circumstances. I thought that being in similar circumstances himself, he could understand how she felt and so could back her more successfully than anyone else. Mr. Young was surprisingly enthusiastic about this proposal and readily agreed to a bedside meeting. Only the Consultant Psychogeriatrician remained and he too agreed, provided we all met first without Mrs. Overton.

Hospitals are rarely equipped for meetings of more than two people, and about ten of us were squeezed into a converted broom cupboard. Mr. Young had also come to the meeting. The geriatrician began by reporting on Mrs. Overton's state of health, which he proclaimed to be vigorous, and also on her self-care abilities, which seemed much greater than had been in evidence at home. Mr. Young began to see this as a preliminary to his mother-in-law's discharge and his wife's collapse so he came in to support her. He did so brilliantly, making an impassioned speech on her behalf (possibly the first ever). Mrs. Young was spellbound and we all jumped when her husband punctuated his closing remarks with loud table-banging. But he hadn't bargained on the competition. Not to be outdone, the consultant psychogeriatrician leapt to his feet, declared in the loudest of voices that no one was to shout in his hospital and ordered Mr. Young off the premises. Mr. Young, dripping and deflated, went. The geriatrician then marched us to Mrs. Overton's bed, told Mrs. Overton she could not go home, told Mrs. Young to confirm this; Mrs. Young apologised to her mother, who told us all to 'bugger off'. She went into residential care a week later. The hospital social worker who arranged the admission to care took over the monitoring and I closed the case.

Two Years Later

Two years later I met Mrs. Young in the high street. It could have been ten years, she looked so aged. It was lunch time. Her arms were full of shopping and she was on her way to see her mother. Her daily routine was work, shopping and a visit to her mother at lunch time, work, home to cook the dinner and then back to visit her mother for the evening. She saw little of her husband and daughter and felt worse off than ever – she thought she had brought it on herself for not keeping her mother at home. I thought I had helped create this situation by not finding a way for Mrs. Young to separate.

I am not sure that we learn very much from our failures, but Mrs. Young and Mrs. Overton came so close to breaking out of their trap that despite the dreadful results, it was still a near-miss.

A Second Chance

It is not often in our work that we get a second shot but eight years later I met Mrs. Young again. I had just become a Consultant to a small, family therapy clinic at a psychiatric day hospital. The first case I was to supervise was of a 59-year-old woman who had been a psychiatric in-patient for nearly two years, had spent a year at the day hospital and showed no signs of improving. Her husband was considered unhelpful to her and she and the staff relied heavily on her sister, who seemed to keep the whole family going. Husband, sister and twenty-four year old daughter had all been invited to a family meeting to discuss future plans for – Mrs. Young!

A few years after I had last seen her, Mrs. Young's mother eventually died. At around the same time so did Mr. Young's mother. Also around this time Mrs. Young's nephew Paul died unexpectedly. Somewhere in all this Mrs. Young had a massive breakdown and was compulsorily admitted to psychiatric hospital where she was heavily sedated. She had soon recovered her reason but behaved in an extremely dependent way, which no treatment had been able to alter. Only her sister seemed to have any influence on her, and the hospital staff were convinced that without her sister's constant care and attention, she would have become almost totally withdrawn – once again a strong sisterly relationship emerges.

The family at this point looked like this:

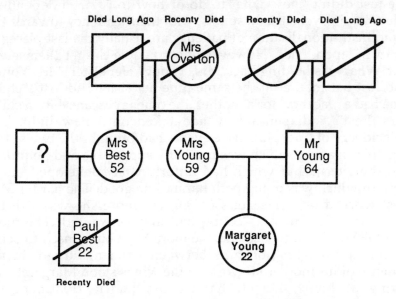

Mr. Young had become much busier at work over the past couple of years and Margaret was engaged – or not. She had broken it off three times already and it looked doubtful that the planned wedding would go ahead.

The Treatment Plan

The hospital were seeing Mrs. Young's mental state as an unresolved grief reaction to the death of her mother. They had been trying to get Mr. Young to support his wife through her pain but had gratefully settled for the sister, who was anyway much closer to Mrs. Young than was her husband. I suggested an alternative view which would lead to a different course of action than was being taken.

I thought Mrs. Young's breakdown was understandable, given the triple bereavement and her great attachment to her mother. I imagined she felt as guilty (and as relieved) about her mother's death as she had about her removal into care and, like camels, we are all limited in the burden we can carry. The more significant feature was Mrs. Young's "stuckness". My assumption was that her failure to separate from her mother had left her dependent – she just didn't know what to do or how to *be* an independent adult. And psychiatric hospitals, with their tendency towards the rapid institutionalisation of patients, are usually the last places to learn independence. However, most people do get themselves out. What was holding back Mrs. Young? Her sister. Mrs. Young had lost her mother at the same time her sister had lost a child. One had a 'vacancy' for a mother, the other a 'vacancy' for a child. Mrs. Best's indispensability had taken on a new light. The coincidence of tragic life-cycle events had brought the two sisters together in a way which was mutually supportive and helpful in the short term, but which had unfortunately developed into a pattern which was doing both families no good. The harder Mrs. Best worked on her sister's behalf, the more she was like the competent parent Mrs. Young had always wanted .The more childlike Mrs. Young became, the more Mr. Young, used to being excluded from relationships between women, turned, in the absence of his mother, to work. In the wings stood Margaret, still living at home, herself having psychiatric treatment for depression, and becoming increasingly uncertain about an independent future. In twenty-five years time would *she* be looking after her mother and wondering about her own future when she died?

There appeared to be a three-fold task to enable Mrs. Young to at last move on in her life. Firstly, she needed to be helped to separate from her 'mother' (her sister); secondly, Mr. Young would need to be encouraged to fill the emotional vacuum such a separation would create – and as this new relationship would be a couple relationship and not a 'parent-child' one, it would demand more equality and independence from Mrs. Young. Finally, Margaret would need to be helped towards her own independence. She would need to experience her mother's *not needing* her. She might then be freer to consider her own future.

The team quickly accommodated this new picture and the action it required, and suggested that Mrs. Best be deterred from attending the meeting, thereby commencing the separation. However, this might have had the opposite effect. Mrs. Best was deeply committed to her sister and had strong views about her care. To be suddenly excluded from such an important meeting would be more likely to pull her further in to the system than it would be to separate the two sisters. Mrs. Best would become suspicious, think her sister was going to be treated badly and double her efforts to protect her. This would be most unhelpful. Much more useful would be to have Mrs. Best at the meeting and experience how she and her sister have become entangled. It is a basic tenet of structural family therapy that problems are dealt with *during* the session. For this to happen the problems must be *enacted*: the family therapist's task is to keep the problem on the boil long enough for the family members to work out a new solution. To help them the therapist might *unbalance* the system a little by siding with different family members at different times.

Unbalancing the System

The plan for this family meeting was to unbalance the system in Mr. Young's favour, at least for a while. The purpose of this was two-fold. Firstly, it seemed important for the couple to re-engage if Mrs. Young were going to lead anything like a normal life. Secondly, we anticipated that any move by Mr. Young towards his wife would jeopardise the relationship between the two sisters; this would make Mrs. Best hang onto her sister, who would be caught in a 'tug of love'. If the therapist pulled with Mr. Young, then there was a chance that the 'parent-child' tie between the sisters would break. We had not yet thought about Margaret but hoped to develop some ideas during the session when we had had a chance to see her reaction to the struggle for her mother. All this does not mean that Mrs. Best was acting in any way malevolent. This approach is based on an idea that systems have a tendency to stay the same, so any attempt to change in one part of the system will lead to counter-change moves in another. Mr. Young's getting closer to his wife would represent an enormous change; his sister-in-law's blocking of this would be the counter-measure designed to neutralise this (just as the psychogeriatrician had inadvertently blocked an earlier attempt by Mr. Young). Another assumption of this model of family therapy (and many others) is that all behaviour, even problem behaviour, serves a function within the system. Certainly Mrs. Young's breakdown had given her sister something to take her mind off her own tragedy and this had enabled Mr. Young to carry on with his half-relationship with his wife. For her part, Margaret, standing in the wings, was saved the worry and risk of striking out on her own.

This was the hypothesis with which the therapist began work. Such hypotheses are neither true nor false, but rather a means of understanding the information available in a way which then gives ideas about what to do. If the resulting action proves beneficial to the family, the hypothesis might be expanded but if it leads nowhere, then a new hypothesis needs to be developed. It is what we do all the time, anyway, but in a more structured and purposeful fashion. In this case the hypothesis proved extremely useful. The therapist had called the meeting *not* for family therapy (because this makes people think they are going to be blamed) but for a planning meeting. And this is what they did. Everyone acknowledged that Mrs. Young's progress had long since come to a halt and everyone accepted that she could not remain forever at the day hospital. At some point sooner rather than later she would have to go home. To do this she would need to build up her confidence. The obvious person to help her was her husband. How?

This was the obvious logic through which the family was led and the question how was put directly to Mr. Young. He was put on the spot. Predictably Mrs. Best came to the rescue and began making suggestions herself. Because this would have kept Mr. Young on the sidelines, she was politely interrupted and Mr. Young again asked how he was going to help his wife grow more confident. He began to come up with suggestions – going out together, helping her shop, going to the pictures. Much of the session was spent pressing for detail about these plans, not allowing them to be vague but wanting to know which shops, which park, which film and when all these events would happen. From one point of view this could look like harassment – Mr. Young being bombarded with question after question but more importantly it was a way of supporting him. It is often by challenging people to produce the best they have, that we actually begin to see the best they have and there is no doubt that Mr. Young grew more enthusiastic about spending time with his wife as the session went on. She responded simply by beginning to glow. Her sister was less convinced. After being silenced she spent much of the session looking disbelievingly at Mr. Young, as if to say that while we might all believe him, she certainly didn't. Margaret remained quiet for the whole session though both she and her aunt were asked a number of questions about how they might contribute to the new developments. Another meeting was set up for a week later with the Youngs having a variety of 'tasks' to accomplish in between.

We thought we had been successful in bringing Mr. and Mrs. Young closer together but were uncertain about Mrs. Best and Margaret. We decided to explore their reactions to the week in more depth. First of all the therapist found out if Mr. and Mrs. Young had actually done some of the things they had planned. They had, in fact, done them all and more, and appeared very close and very pleased with themselves. Margaret said she had been depressed all week and was thinking of calling off her wedding. She too was responding to the change by trying to pull back. If her parents became independent they would not need her to look after them, which would mean she would have to become independent herself. If she became ill she might distract her parents from their new course in life and bring things back to 'normal'. Maybe! Mrs. Best had been feeling low, too. She had been thinking about her son. This was a very good sign because it was likely to mean that she was already loosening her ties with her sister. Our interest in the aunt and niece led to a most moving discussion. They talked of Paul, who was, apparently, an extremely gifted and likeable young man. He and Margaret had been like brother and sister and, indeed, they had been treated more like son and daughter by both sets of parents. As Margaret described his qualities, she suddenly broke into tears and said that his death was so unfair – he was the one with a real life ahead of him and she was just wasting hers. She then said quite from the heart that she wished it was her not him and told how guilty she felt with her aunt for still being alive. This was said without drama and it shocked everyone. Mrs. Best, who was sitting beside Margaret, drew her into her arms saying she had never begrudged Margaret her life, never even thought it might have been her rather than Paul who died. She declared her love for her niece while they both sobbed in each other's arms.

The Honeymoon

As the temperature cooled and the meeting moved back towards planning Mr. and Mrs. Young's next steps, it became clear that the balance of the whole family had shifted. Mr. Young no longer needed pressing to think of things to do with his wife; Mrs. Best no longer looked sceptical and instead encouraged their plan-making. Margaret wondered about putting her wedding off to give her parents more time to sort out their lives. Her aunt then offered to help Margaret make the wedding arrangements so Margaret would not be disadvantaged. Everybody was happy and Mrs. Young's discharge was planned for one month's time. There would be another family meeting just before, and the self-selected task chosen by Mr. Young was to arrange not a second but a first honeymoon holiday for himself and his wife.

Whether or not the hypotheses had been right, they had certainly been effective in helping the therapist pursue a line of thought and questions which led the family to make new discoveries and decide new courses of action.

In effect the uniting of Mr. and Mrs. Young had initially threatened the position of Mrs. Best and Margaret. But they then discovered that they had matching needs. Mrs. Best was again mourning her son but still had some spare parenting capacity which she transferred from her sister to her niece. Margaret, too, wanted a parent but one who could help launch her into her own life. Her aunt, who had been like a parent anyway, could do this for her.

A month later they all came back. The wedding was still going ahead. Margaret and Mrs. Best were both enthusiastic about this, and Margaret looked both older and more alive. Mr. and Mrs. Young were like a courting couple with secret looks and giggles. It was clear that the wedding would be theirs, too! They had been leading a very active life, with Mrs. Young hardly attending the day hospital in the last two weeks. Their 'honeymoon' plans had been kept a secret until their formal announcement at the meeting. They let the suspense build up, gleeful at everyone's anticipation, and then told us they were going to Margate to spend two weeks with the couple who had fostered Mr. Young when he was an evacuee during the war!

They had found new parents but ones well -practised in letting children go. Mrs. Young has received no psychiatric treatment since her discharge (and honeymoon) five years ago. Mr. Young will have retired and hopefully the couple will enjoy in their later years a degree of independence and autonomy which they were never able to achieve as young and middle-aged adults.

CHAPTER 6

DECLARATIONS OF WAR

Triangles

One of my areas of study as a student was social psychology, most of which I forgot within the hour, but two bits stayed with me. Yerk constructed a Y-shaped box with worm-food at the end of one branch and an electrified screen at the other.

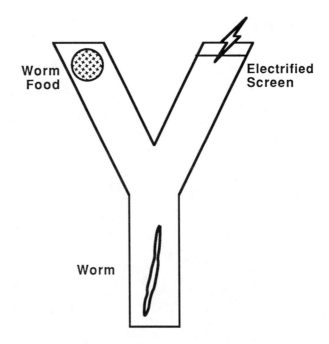

YERK'S WORM EXPERIMENT

He put a worm in the tail of the Y. After receiving its first electric shock, the worm always chose the route which led to its food. I have never found a use for this information. The other thing I remember is Heider's Balance Theory, which I found immensely useful for a long time. While preparing this chapter I looked up

Heider's original 1946 paper[3] and realised my memory had done a most effective job of editing his ideas. They also appear in Lyn Hoffman's *Foundations of Family Therapy* (see the reading guide at the end of this book) but, again, are too complex for my use. I present them here in my own ultra-simplified state which is the way they can be most readily used to help sort out problems while at the same time being so over-simple, they can easily be discarded by those who don't like doing things 'by numbers'. Heider broke the social world down into four basic triangular relationships – two balanced and two unbalanced. The assumption for the purposes of my version is that each triangle represents a permanent set of relationships – no one can walk out of the door. For our purposes (and this shows it is only a theory) each party to the relationship is equal.

The Three Musketeers

The first balanced triangle is one in which everyone gets on well together:

A and B get on, B and C get on, and C and A get on equally well.

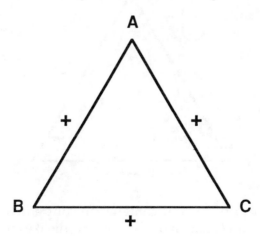

---

[3] Heider F. 'Attitudes and Cognitive Organisation' *Journal of Psychology* 21 (1946)

This is a strong positive set of relationships, each reinforcing the other two. Where threesomes like this exist families, work places, classrooms, and friendship groups, they usually make a formidable power base. This can be tested by drawing lines between all members of a group who regularly interact: assign a positive value to all those relationships where people get on well and a negative value to those who are in conflict or even *might* be in potential conflict. Consider the influence on the whole group of any positively relating threesome. Such threesomes often make powerful forces!

But it's Unfair

The second balanced triangle is one in which two have united against one.

A gets on well with B while C and B and A and C have a mutual antipathy.

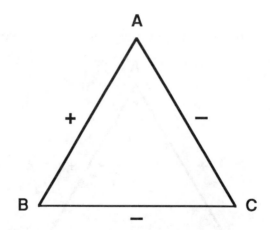

This is balanced because it contains no contradictions. A and B like each other and share a dislike for C; C dislikes them both, and their liking for each other confirms C's opinion of them. There are familiar playground relationships in which three friends alternate as the odd one out. The plus and minuses move round the triangle as alliances are made and broken, but the basic balance – two against one – remains the same. When the positions remain fixed, it can have more sinister implications: A and B scapegoating

C or if C has more power than A and B, it can be a situation of an elite oppressing a majority, as with apartheid and slavery. Where this configuration remains static in a work situation, it is a sign of an oppressive manager (if C has the power) or a scapegoated colleague. Neither situation is constructive or productive of good work. Where the likes and dislikes move around the triangle, it is likely to represent straight forward office politics (and other relationships).

The next two triangles are *unbalanced*.

Guess Who's Coming to Dinner

Where one person likes two others but they don't like each other, great discomfort is felt when the three have to be in one another's presence. Who hasn't invited two good friends to dinner and found that they simply hate each other; or who hasn't spent a family Christmas with two members who dislike each other – perhaps a husband and brother both loved by the same woman.

B and C dislike one another, but both like and are liked by A.

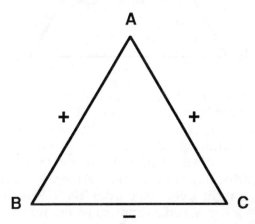

These situations are so uncomfortable, we tend to avoid them but if we can't, we try to change them into a balanced form. It is in the nature of unbalanced triangles to try to move to a balanced state. The woman caught between her brother and her husband will feel each pressing her to take his side and eventually (if she cannot vent her exasperation by leaving) is likely to side with one against the other, if only for the time being. This will then create a two against one triangle. Later she might feel sorry for the one left out and make up to him, even at the expense of getting into a new conflict with the other. So it goes on with the final variation being the two men getting together against the woman. *Eastenders*, *Coronation Street* and just about every other 'soap' are based on recurring series of just such triangles.

A Sort of Hell

The last of the four triangles, also unbalanced, represents a set of relationships in which no one gets anything – a sort of hell.

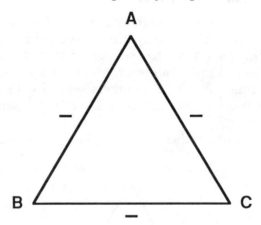

There is no reason for this relationship to exist and if its participants cannot break away, they will seek to form an alliance to create a two against one situation. Post-war world politics have a number of memorable examples: the China-Russia-America triangle was a three-way conflict with constant attempts by one party to take advantage of the other. America would woo China while China fought over its border with Russia; Russia and America have now reached a rapprochement which allows both to condemn China. At a more local but no less significant level, the ambiguous position of the Palestinians in world politics – sometimes accepted, sometimes not – shows how unstable three way conflicts are and how high a price will be paid to find a balance. At a family level such a situation might be one in which a couple takes on the care of an elderly parent which proves too much. They begin to row, first with each other and then with the parent. The three-way fight is impossible to maintain and so they begin taking sides – two against one.

The importance of Heider's balance theory is not as a theory of relationships, but as a theory about the relationship *between* relationships – the relationship that any two people have (A and B) will always have an influence on their relationship with a third person (A and C, B and C). This is one of the central tenets of systems theory and offers an explanation of how we as professionals can influence clients' lives without necessarily having direct contact. This influence, which passes back and forth between client and professionals, is well documented in the field of child protection where the professional network has to be very active. In child sexual abuse cases, where hidden conflicts and secrets abound, there will nearly always be an outbreak of serious conflict and a withholding of information at some point during the investigation and follow-up. Similarly in cases of physical abuse, it is not uncommon to find the professionals fighting over the best course of action and losing patience with each other. These are normal processes, and when professionals are working well together, they are soon recognised for what they are and no lasting damage is done. Similar disputes arise with older people, particularly those about whom professionals have special concerns.

I once found myself in dispute with a housing manager about an elderly client who was in two minds about where he wanted to live. The client's behaviour alternated from kindliness to downright rudeness. The dispute culminated in a professional's and resident's meeting – my client declined to attend. Half a dozen professionals and over twenty residents gathered in a small hall and gave vent to their feelings. About half the group were against my client and wanted him moved, while the rest just as vociferously defended him. The meeting was inconclusive, but no complaints were received for a year. I then found myself arguing with a new housing manager and eventually a second meeting took place. More or less the same people attended and exactly the same positions were taken, the only difference being that most people had swapped sides! The end product was the same – the complaints, and apparently the behaviour causing them, ceased.

My client had attended neither meeting, and did not want to know what had taken place, yet his relationship with other tenants changed significantly.

The following accounts show how this phenomenon, the way relationships affect one another, can be used in the solving of the most intractable of problems.

THE STORY OF MISS PROUDFOOT

Miss Proudfoot was a fighter. Life had not been kind to her but she had not allowed this to stop her getting on with it. As she grew into old age, she remained a fighter, guarding her independence while at the same time demanding a high standard of service. Not everyone found her easy but she had developed, over a number of years, a very close, supportive relationship with a social worker. This social worker was able to help her through periodic crises and acted as her advocate in obtaining the services of other professionals. Most recently, after several months of hard bargaining, the social worker had secured for Miss Proudfoot a flat in a sheltered housing block – something they both viewed as a major achievement. What followed will be an all too familiar story.

Within three months the warden was reporting almost nightly disturbances by Miss Proudfoot. These included knocking on neighbours' doors in the early hours, ringing the alarm bell for trivial reasons, apparent disorientation and unclean habits. This was not the picture of Miss Proudfoot painted by the social worker to the admission panel, and the warden felt extremely aggrieved about the 'misrepresentation' of Miss Proudfoot's capacities.

The social worker thought the warden must be exaggerating, after all Miss Proudfoot had done none of these things before. An affronted warden then began to keep a daily record of all Miss Proudfoot's 'transgressions' to prove to the social worker that her complaints were justified.

The social worker, fearful for her client's future should she lose her flat, put forward 'reasons' for the behaviour and tried to convince the warden that she was being too harsh. The warden grew increasingly impatient with a social worker who didn't have to live with the problem, who didn't have sixty other residents to think of and whose sleep wasn't being disturbed almost every night. Miss Proudfoot's future looked bleak and the only positive factor was that, against all the odds, the social worker had maintained a good relationship with Miss Proudfoot. But as is so often the case, a good relationship with one's client does not necessarily solve the problem.

What gives rise to such a situation? It could be many things – something overlooked when preparing Miss Proudfoot for her move, not noticing that Miss Proudfoot was less keen on moving than she appeared, or possibly just the shock of the move. Who can anticipate exactly what effects such a major event will have on someone's sense of equilibrium? Miss Proudfoot, not the easiest of people to deal with, may have 'got off on the wrong foot' with the warden and not been able to use the help she had come for; or she may have seen that help as a threat to her freedom and so rejected it at the time she most needed it.

There are many factors which might lead to this state of affairs and good practice, close liaison and co-operation notwithstanding, there will always be unpredictable factors, and we will always need to be able to deal with crises like the one facing Miss Proudfoot and those engaged with her. It was not long before the social worker felt in an impossible dilemma and expressed this as: "How can I persuade the warden to keep Miss Proudfoot? And if I fail, how can I persuade Miss Proudfoot to accept residential care?" Everything indicated that both these aims were lost causes: the warden had so far not been persuaded and every attempt to do so had only increased her resolve to have Miss Proudfoot moved; for her part, Miss Proudfoot was showing no signs of changing her life's behaviour pattern of resisting other people's attempts to direct her life.

The social worker had, therefore, posed a question in a form which precluded all possibility of a satisfactory answer. She could neither persuade the warden nor the client and was therefore trapped by her own question. When it happens that a problem is presented in an insoluble form, and it happens frequently in the intricate pathways of community care, the first step must always be to restate the problem. In this case the original form was: "How can I persuade....?" To reformulate the problem it would be necessary to ask the purpose of this persuasion. In the first instance, the purpose is to enable Miss Proudfoot to stay in her flat. The 'new' problem might therefore be: "How can I help Miss Proudfoot stay in her flat?" To begin with the answer to this is a 'don't know' but at least this allows for the *possibility* of a solution, whereas the 'persuasion' question offered no such possibility and was even making matters worse.

On the face of it, this process of going back on a question is as simple as turning back from a dead end in a maze, but many a client's – and many a worker's – difficulty is that they don't turn back but keep on trying the same solution – like a car stuck in sand, the harder you work the engine, the deeper the wheels sink. The warden and the social worker had been doing just this, going on with a 'bad' solution until it escalated into something harder to solve than the original problem.

So how can the social worker help Miss Proudfoot stay in her flat? Trying to persuade the warden to think differently is making the warden more determined to ignore the social worker. That is working against Miss Proudfoot's chances, so the first step must be to stop trying to persuade the warden. On the other hand, agreeing with the warden might be an even quicker way of losing Miss Proudfoot her flat, so that does not seem a good idea either. Not trying to persuade and not agreeing with the warden are, therefore, two necessary 'ingredients' for a possible solution.

Applying Heider's balance theory to this situation, we have a two-against-one-triangle:

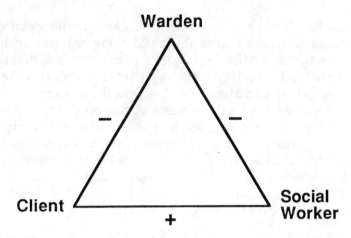

Both the social worker and the client are in conflict with the warden while maintaining a positive relationship between themselves. This is an interesting situation because on the face of it there is nothing to worry about – it is the warden who looks to be in the weak position and as the triangle is balanced, it will remain steady indefinitely. However, in this situation not all participants have equal power. It is the warden who ultimately decides who can stay and who must leave. This decision might have to go through a number of channels but if it takes too long, then an overburdened warden can simply decide one evening that she is *not* going to pick her tenant up, or calm her down herself, but is going to call an ambulance instead. It can be very difficult for some people to get back into their own homes from hospital, if they lose the support of key professionals.

So, Miss Proudfoot was vulnerable. Her behaviour had reached a sufficiently worrying quality to justify calling for medical help in an emergency and as if reflecting this, the relationship between warden and social worker was equally at odds. Only Miss Proudfoot and the social worker were getting on together – even in these desperate circumstances, or as the social worker said, *because* of these desperate circumstances, the good relationship needed to be maintained. If it wasn't, Miss Proudfoot would have no one.

The solution to this problem was so shocking to the social worker, it was several weeks before she could come to terms with it and then only because Miss Proudfoot's behaviour had deteriorated still further. The social worker's main task was to change the relationship between Miss Proudfoot and the warden, to change it from a negative to a positive value. Attempts to change her own relationship with the warden had failed and in any case could prove dangerous to Miss Proudfoot (if the warden and social worker started to agree). The only other relationship over which the social worker had a *direct* influence was that between herself and Miss Proudfoot. What impact would changing this relationship have on the system as a whole?

The suggestion to the social worker that she 'pick a fight' with her client was designed to set in motion a process of change which offered Miss Proudfoot at least some chance of continued independence. The idea of creating a conflict between social worker and client was intended to create an unbalanced system:

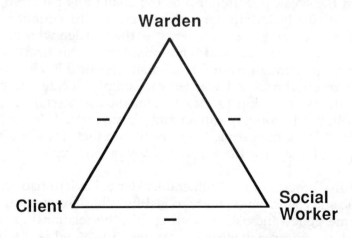

Client–warden, social worker–warden and social worker–client would all be in conflict. This state of imbalance would create pressure within the system to change to a more balanced state – one of the negative relationships would have to go positive to create the two-against-one balance. Here the social worker's position was the key. As long as she maintained her conflict with both warden and client, the only relationship free to change would be that between Miss Proudfoot and the warden. It was important to anticipate the difficulty the social worker would have in maintaining this position because she would be subject to as much pressure to change as the others. She held her ground by treating client and warden with the deepest respect.

To Miss Proudfoot she acknowledged their long-standing relationship, her admiration of Miss Proudfoot's independent spirit, the real difficulty Miss Proudfoot was experiencing in having to adjust her ways to more communal living; and she declared their history strong enough to withstand some straight-forward honesty. She then found that she had much to be annoyed about this very capable woman throwing away her chance of continuing an independent life. Both women had words to say and the hardest thing of all was for the social worker not to 'kiss and make up'! Instead, she left Miss Proudfoot to think on her position, while promising to think herself on what Miss Proudfoot had said.

To the warden the social worker also acknowledged their long standing relationship, their many shared clients over the years and the value she had always placed on the warden's judgement. She also acknowledged the warden's twenty-four-hour task, as opposed to her own seven or eight hours, but stuck to her position that the warden was wrong over Miss Proudfoot. But instead of trying to persuade the warden to change, she respected her position and simply agreed to differ. Again, the hardest part was resisting the warden's response 'to bury the hatchet'. She left, respecting the warden, but very sorry that she had chosen this particular course of action. The social worker continued to maintain this conflict within a protective framework of respect for two or three weeks. Each contact with warden or client put pressure on her to change – but if *she* changed, it would mean either a return to the original position or to one in which she and the warden would unite against Miss Proudfoot. It was therefore crucial that she remained in conflict; and eventually it began to pay off. The social worker started to notice a lessening in the degree of complaints about each other which she heard from Miss Proudfoot and the warden. It became even harder then to maintain the conflict, but she at least kept some of it going – there is always something clients and professionals, and professionals and professionals, can disagree about!

The triangle was shifting to a new balance, two against one, but this time the alliance was between warden and client. Over the next few weeks Miss Proudfoot and the warden developed a way of being together which was hardly friendship, but at least involved each respecting the other's way of life. As their relationship improved, and because of it, Miss Proudfoot's behaviour became less bizarre and less troublesome. Her confusion abated and she returned to being something much closer to her old self. Eventually there was nothing to maintain a conflict about, and what remained was a three-sided relationship of mutual respect. Miss Proudfoot was off the 'danger list'.

I drew two important lessons from this case. Firstly, the influence of relationships on relationships – changing one's own relationship with a person can have a direct effect on relationships with others. This idea crops up throughout family therapy: for instance, the effect of the change in Mr. and Mrs. Young's relationship on that between Mrs. Best and Margaret. Heider offers a simple 'ready reckoner' starting point to understanding this process and also a way of *predicting* the effects of a change in one part of the system on the other parts. It must, however, be remembered that it is only one way of looking at relationships and does not contain any real truths. If it helps, as with Miss Proudfoot, then it is useful; if it doesn't help, then it is meaningless. This is also a very simplified version, so at best can only provide a crude guide to action.

The second and more fundamental lesson is how dangerous to clients our good relationships with them can sometimes be. The good relationship between Miss Proudfoot and the social worker seemed all that was between her and complete isolation, yet it was this very relationship which was holding the more dangerous conflict in place. Clients, particularly older clients, are tough. They often have more experience and have had more tests of survival

CHAPTER 4

MORE THAN ENOUGH

SERVICES AND CARE

Doris Lessing gives a most vivid description of a home help's task in her *Diary of Jane Somers* and some of her fictional characters may well have met the characters in this account. Though cleaning is the main task, caring is the main function, and home helps are the mainstay of most community care programmes. In my five years managing a home care team I know of at least two instances where home helps have paid for their client's funeral to avoid a council burial, and each week saw an abundance of less dramatic signs of care and commitment. But while home helps and other daily carers of older people provide the bulk of care, they cannot be responsible for all of it and even the best home helps have dissatisfied customers.

One cause of dissatisfaction can be nobody's fault. As people grow older they may not only lose some of their physical and mental abilities, but are as likely to lose family and friends, sometimes to the point of having no one in the world to care for them in their own right. Isolation is perhaps the single most common problem for older people, and when family and friends are absent and neighbourliness is not available, there are precious few ways in which an older person can experience care. Clubs and day centres are invaluable in this respect, but they hold nothing for those unused to or unsympathetic to this form of socialising. What is left are services such as home helps, meals-on-wheels, district nursing, occupational therapy and social work. Each of these is intended to meet a particular need with only the social worker having a more generalised function. But even here there is limited scope. A social worker needs to know what the client's needs are and rarely has much more time than that needed to act as broker for other services. To all intents and purposes, if an older person without family or friends needs to be cared for, that caring must be channelled through one of the limited number of community services. Though professional caring can never be a real substitute for the care of family and friends, it is usually

Kelleher and the home help against the occupational therapist and Miss Kelleher and the nurses against the occupational therapist). This would have been no great problem except that Miss Kelleher's general physical and emotional health started to deteriorate with some speed. The wardens, from their more distant position, were able to notice this and described Miss Kelleher as becoming more depressed and more demanding. It seemed that this last set-back to her health had seriously challenged her self-confidence, and as independence was vital to her, the sudden loss had led her to think the worst. The well-intentioned help given by the home help and nurses was, in fact, increasing her sense of dependence and therefore feeding her despondency. They were also neutralising the occupational therapist's attempts to get Miss Kelleher to start fighting again.

A letter of complaint (written in the most beautiful, firm handwriting) from Miss Kelleher about the occupational therapist's refusal to provide the mechanical feeding equipment provided a convenient reason to call a conference, and Miss Kelleher agreed to host it. The days leading up to this meeting revealed some surprising information: the nurses and the home help were all fed up with Miss Kelleher and felt overwhelmed by her. They shared this with each other, but not with the occupational therapist or with Miss Kelleher.

I made a point of beginning the meeting by asking for a 'cards-on-the-table' discussion in which everyone would be honest. Miss Kelleher endorsed this, saying in a voice of considerable authority that she demanded nothing less. However, when it came to the feeding issue, she assumed a very different mien, appearing small, frail and helpless. The home help and nurses then admitted how difficult it was for them to say 'no'. If they weren't persuaded by Miss Kelleher's authority, they found themselves being caught out by her vulnerability. For her part Miss Kelleher could not quite keep the look of satisfaction off her face as this group of professionals admitted their weakness! The main part of the meeting took the form of the occupational therapist explaining all her reasons for not recommending the feeding device. Everyone was then encouraged to question her in great detail and to put counter-arguments. As it happened everyone, except Miss

Kelleher, ended up agreeing with the occupational therapist, but not all were confident that they could resist Miss Kelleher's powers of persuasion.

Here I assumed my role as a manager (sometimes it can be useful!) and first of all stated my respect for the occupational therapist and my duty to back up her professional judgement, provided it had been subject to rigorous testing. I then turned to the nurses, admitting that I had no authority over them but, nevertheless, demanding as one professional to another that they did not interfere in the sphere of competency of another professional. Any future interference would merit a formal complaint. This sounds very heavy-handed but because the meeting had been conducted in a very respectful way towards all members and because the statement was couched in very formal language, it was not experienced as inflammatory. Similarly so with the home help, whom I threatened with disciplinary action if she exceeded her duties by feeding Miss Kelleher. Had I got my tone even slightly wrong, I could easily have sparked off an industrial action, but the home help, too, accepted my unusual intervention as a counter-authority to that of Miss Kelleher. She could now draw on that authority to say 'no' to Miss Kelleher's requests to be fed. Finally I turned to Miss Kelleher, who had conducted herself extremely well during most of the meeting. I told her some of the things I had heard about her past accomplishments, pointed to the command she had over a group of very experienced professionals as proof of her power as a person, respected her wish to have her own way, but reiterated my intention to support the professional judgement of the occupational therapist. My last words were: "And so, Miss Kelleher, it is with great sadness and great regret, and a wish that things could be different, but even with all my respect for you I have no choice but to declare war – may the best person win!"

Everyone was silent until I left. I don't know what they did then, but within a few weeks Miss Kelleher was back to her old self, still fighting but no longer depressed. The nurses went back to visiting in ones only, and the home help (who later sought me out to say what an interesting meeting it had been) felt much less burdened by Miss Kelleher. The occupational therapist and Miss Kelleher continued to argue over what Miss Kelleher could reasonably manage herself, but the arguments no longer blocked constructive activity. When two years later Miss Kelleher's arthritis took another turn for the worse, and we all decided that to be fed by the home help would be more dignified than trying to operate a mechanical shovel, and Miss Kelleher accepted this increased dependence without her previous fall into depression. What had been important was to recognise and honour Miss Kelleher's fighting spirit. The occupational therapist had tried but had been outnumbered by the rest of the professional network. My virtual declaration of war on the professionals had made me a suitably worthy opponent for Miss Kelleher, while at the same time giving the others permission not to agree with her every request. To Miss Kelleher the declaration was a clear sign that she was still alive and kicking. Once again, not being 'nice' was exactly what was required.

CHAPTER 7

SAILING TO BYZANTIUM AND OTHER STORIES

BREAKING THE SILENCE

This is a story of Saleha Bibi, a twenty-three year old woman who helped us find a way of speaking with people without voices. She could not speak. No one knew for certain what she could understand, though most people thought she could understand something. She was paralysed from the neck down and was entirely dependent on others for all her bodily functions.

Her mother, whom she lived with, had recently had a hysterectomy and was suffering from very severe back pain. She had one sister living at home and another nearby; her father was dead. The family came from Bangladesh but there was no local Bengali community: they had moved to their flat because it was adapted for wheelchair use.

The family had managed to care for Saleha with virtually no assistance until quite recently. Then in the space of two years, Mrs. Bibi's husband had died, her eldest daughter had married and moved away, and she herself began to suffer poor health. They came to the notice of the home care team because of a referral for residential care (we had instituted a policy that all referrals of adults for care must be assessed by the home care team, not always popular with the other teams, but the only way to *guarantee* a serious look at alternatives).

When we met the family (a field social worker and an occupational therapist made the first contact), we found the family in a desperate state and unable to think of any solution to their difficulty other than residential care. Mrs. Bibi had been told that she needed an operation, which would leave her unable to do any lifting for at least six months, and she was already weak. Her other daughter was at college, which was important to all of them, and Saleha needed constant attention. They all wanted Saleha to stay at home and as far as we could make out, Saleha wanted this, too.

The upshot was that after some extremely hard bargaining, a number of meetings, some financial juggling and a great deal of good will, funding was provided for a live-in volunteer. Nevertheless it was a bit slow for Mrs. Bibi, who had to have her operation before the final arrangements were made, meaning that Saleha did after all go into residential care for about a month. The volunteer lasted about a month, too. She reported on a family in a permanent state of conflict with Saleha at the centre, often being shouted at and sometimes being hit. The volunteer and Mrs. Bibi soon fell out, and while the outward trappings of civility were maintained, they grew to hate each other. It was a surprise that the relationship lasted as long as it did. Unfortunately, as is often the case with new situations in which a great deal is invested, it can be difficult to acknowledge the fact that it isn't working. It was only a few days before the volunteer walked out that we knew the scale of the problem. As a temporary measure we moved three home helps in with the family to provide almost twenty-four hour cover. (A lot of homes went uncleaned for the next two weeks, so we had a lot of making up to do with our other clients). We then called an emergency meeting at Mrs. Bibi's home. To this came the social worker, the occupational therapist, the home help organiser, two of the home helps, our own volunteer organiser and volunteer, the co-ordinator of the volunteer agency providing the live-in person, a worker from the respite care residential home and a district nurse who had become involved. Mrs. Bibi and her three daughters were also present. I had not met the family but was brought in to chair the meeting.

There was a great deal to be said: Mrs. Bibi wanted everyone to know exactly how much care and attention Saleha needed: her married daughter wanted everyone to realise that they weren't doing enough: the volunteer co-ordinator wanted to know exactly what pressures the last volunteer had been under and whether it would be the same for a new volunteer; the nurse wanted to know if Saleha had really been hit. As a meeting it had all the makings of a disaster and the casualty would be Saleha, who sat in her wheelchair with a grin on her face and her head flopping. And if Saleha were hurt, so, too, would be her family.

I had at that time just read a paper with an impossible title by four Italians with just as impossible names[4] which was to turn out to be a landmark in the development of family therapy and set out the basis for what became known as the Milan Model of family therapy[5]. What occurred to me as I watched the meeting revolving around the silent Saleha was how the Milan team dealt with an absent member in a family meeting. What was happening in the room was a discussion about who should care for Saleha, and where and how they would do it. When a person doesn't speak, however hard we try not to, we start speaking across them, about them and even for them and they start to become invisible. I found that if I looked at Saleha in a way that I could actually see her, then everyone else, and the discussion they were having, faded into a blur. On the other hand, if I began tuning into the discussion and thought about speaking myself, Saleha began to disappear. So I thought that the way the Milan team 'included' an absent person could be used just as effectively to include a non-speaking person. Breaking into the meeting I asked:

Me: Mrs. Bibi, if Saleha *could* speak and I were to ask her to choose someone to speak for her at this meeting, who do you think she would choose?

Mrs. Bibi: (*after long thought*) I think she would choose Muni (*the younger daughter*).

Me: Do you also think she would choose you, Muni, or do you think she might choose someone else?

Muni: I would have said she would choose Mother.

Mrs. Bibi: No, you and she have an understanding ...

Mani: (*the eldest daughter*) I think she would choose Muni, too. They've always been close even though they do argue.

---

4   Selvini-Palazzoli M., Boscolo L., Cecchin J., Prata J. 'Hypothesising, Circularity and Neutrality: Three Guidelines for the Conducting of a Session' *Family Process* 21 (1980)

5   Probably the best current introduction to family therapy is John Burnham's book *Family Therapy* which is based on the Milan Model (See Reading List).

Just as the Milan team's paper was going to change the family therapy world, these two questions changed this family – or began a process of change which led to a satisfactory resolution of the current difficulty and laid the foundation for a more manageable life ahead.

By answering the questions Mrs. Bibi and her daughters accepted three possibilities: that Saleha can *think* (to understand the questions), that Saleha can *choose*, and that she can *express* her choice. Thinking, choosing and exercising that choice are three of the fundamental characteristics of being a *human being*. Whether or not we always manage to keep these characteristics we can never know, since we experience only the outward expression of others. However, once we treat someone as *not* having these qualities, we treat them as being *less* than human, a degrading experience for both parties. In the meeting with the Bibi family Saleha was becoming 'invisible' because we had been unable to find a way to actively think of and treat her as a thinking, choosing person. These two 'Milan' questions, and the answers given restored to Saleha these basic human qualities.

The new agreement between her mother and her sisters' made the next step easy. If they had disagreed more forcefully, I would have asked more about the differences but in this case I went on:

T	So, Muni, will you agree to be Saleha's 'voice' for this meeting?
Muni	Yes.
T	Well, what I'd like you to do is when I want to ask Saleha a question, I want you to answer as if you were Saleha. Will you be able to do that?
Muni	But I might not get it right.
T	No, I'm sure you won't get it right all the time because you're a different person but I'd still like you to do it. Will you?
Muni	Yes.
T	It will mean that sometimes you'll have to speak twice, once for Saleha and once for yourself. (*Everyone laughs*).

I then spoke to Saleha. I did not know if she could understand – she had such severe disabilities her intelligence was not testable.

T Saleha, your sister is going to speak for you but because she is not you, she might not get it right. If she does get it right, would you lean your head towards her and, if not, lean your head towards your mother (*she was sitting between the two*), and I'll ask her to try speaking for you.

The meeting then progressed at a much slower, more even pace. To begin with Saleha's head seemed to roll randomly and we asked both sister and mother to speak for her. But as time went on Saleha gained more control of her head and began using it very emphatically. She clearly knew everything that was going on and had views about it. What eventually came out was that she had mixed feelings about being at home. She had missed her family when in care but had also enjoyed herself and thought she would like to go back. She had not liked the live-in volunteer because she had not shown proper respect for her mother, but at the same time she had generated much of the disagreement. She was angry at her mother for being unable to care for her and she was also angry because she didn't get enough attention. She sometimes provoked her mother into hitting her (for example, by wetting her bed straight after being taken to the lavatory) just to get a response. She was seen by her mother and sisters as wielding immense power, almost enough to stop her elder sister getting married. She enjoyed and didn't enjoy this power: it was a way of being part of things, but a largely negative way. Different ways were thought about which included some respite. Saleha had thought of care or home as an either/or, when in fact she could have *both* care *and* home. With the new understanding, acknowledgement about difficulties and the need for close contact and support, a new live-in volunteer was agreed along with one week in four at the residential home. As we left the family home Saleha spoke. It was unintelligible to the professionals, but to the family it was a clear 'goodbye'. She had had her own voice all along!

I think it is likely that Saleha understood everything that went on in the meeting, but I don't know; and even if she hadn't, it would have arrived at the same conclusions, since they were conclusions reached by other people. The difference was that these other people had found a way to actively take Saleha into account, Saleha as a person in her own right, and therefore the conclusions reached were conclusions based on the assumption and *experience* of her as a thinking, choosing and participating person.

BEATING PAIN AND DEPRESSION

In work with older people we often meet clients suffering great pain or depression. Often these people 'bear up' and don't complain, but some complain a lot and even the most compassionate of professionals gets fed up with it. We might sit for an hour-and-a-half listening to the same old catalogue of complaints, having months since given up all attempts to help the person do something about their situation; or we might try to look on the bright side and point out the good things that are happening, becoming more frustrated in the process. We might even become firm and say that unless the client is prepared to start doing something about the problem, we will have to stop visiting. Sometimes none of these approaches works and they might even make things worse. What is happening?

One thing that might be happening is that the client is not being heard or is not experiencing himself or herself as being heard. If we are not heard we tend to shout louder: if our story is not being heard we tell it louder and in more detail: if our pain isn't being heard we amplify it – or some people do. If the amplified message is not heard, then the process is likely to reoccur and very soon within that relationship is created a 'complainer' and a 'complained to'. If a client is labelled a complainer, then other professionals come to expect it and might easily switch off. If the client doesn't expect to be heard, he or she might not notice the occasions when a person *does* hear, and so the reputation as a complainer is endorsed even by people who have listened and heard. It is a terrible trap for professionals but a worse one for clients, and it is good for both to escape it.

One way of breaking into this pattern is to assume the client is not telling the whole story. In a sense this has to be the case because if the whole story were told, or sufficient to make sense of the whole communication, then it would be heard. The other side of not being heard is that you are not telling it in a way it can be heard. But it's no use criticising a client for not telling their story right – it would only undermine them further. Their telling needs to be challenged on their own terms. If their terms are to list twenty-five major causes of their depression and they are not being heard, then assume that they are holding back. This might be done in several ways:

> Mr. Smith, because I'm not you I can never fully understand how bad things are for you, but I would like to get as close as I can and I think I'm missing something. Is it me or are you holding back? Is there something you're not telling me, something even worse?

> Mrs. Jones, many people don't talk about their pain because they're embarrassed or they don't trust people to listen and be sympathetic, but you are someone who can get it off your chest. Even so, I'm not sure you're telling me how bad it really is. Is it because you think I won't understand?

> Mr. Brown, I don't think you're being straight with me. You have all these qualities like speaking up for yourself, not letting people walk all over you or take you for granted; you've organised all these things for yourself and yet you're so terribly, terribly unhappy. I don't think you're letting on. In fact, I think things might be a lot worse than you are saying.

The essence of these questions is that they contain an essential truth as understood by the person asking them but the truth has been translated from the language of the asker to that of the asked. This is the art (and the ethic) of communication. It is an art to appreciate the nuances of another's way of talking, and to show that appreciation by adopting some of these nuances is how friendships are made. We do it all the time. The ethics of the matter are to do with respect for others and ultimately human rights. The more different we are from someone through gender, class, culture, race, country, or language the more different are our rules and patterns of communication. To *hear* someone becomes more difficult and requires effort. If we are more powerful than another we can dismiss them by not hearing. British colonialism is an example on a massive scale of one culture not hearing another – the message was, 'If you want to be heard learn our language'. So much of the world was not and still isn't heard. With clients it is we professionals who have the power. But we also have a duty to hear our clients. If this means adopting their ways of saying things, entering into their view of the world rather than imposing ours, then we have a responsibility to do so.

People who repeatedly shout their complaints (or complain in other ways we find difficult to hear) are almost invariably people who are not being heard. To hear them we must accept their language. When a 'shouting' client is encouraged to 'shout louder', that client knows he has the professional's ear. And often clients do shout louder – they have been holding back, there is something they haven't said and it might take hours to say it. It must be listened to and the same questions asked again, the same 'invitation' given. Until the client says 'stop'. This happens when the client is finally sure he or she has been heard; the response will then be a variation on: "No, it's not as bad as that". I think we probably all do it sometime. I remember as a young man I suffered a very painful form of arthritis and was eventually admitted to hospital for a short period. It was such a relief to me that I was being taken seriously (as I saw it) that the whole world looked up, and I began to talk not about the pain but about what it didn't stop me doing. When clients feel heard they too stop having to flag up their pain or whatever is consuming them and can begin to look at other things. As we shall see in the last chapter, looking at these other things can of itself be extremely curative.

SAILING TO BYZANTIUM

A community psychiatric nurse and I went to see a couple in their eighties, referred by the local hospital for marital work. Mr. Doran had been violent to his wife when she visited him during a recent stay. We arrived and were welcomed but when we explained we had come because of their marital problems, they both fell about laughing. They had had over fifty years of extreme happiness together. His shouting and lashing out at her was while under the influence of some medication which hadn't suited him. But they were not without worries, Mrs. Doran being especially concerned that her husband seemed to be giving up on life. We undertook to try to help them, but Mrs. Doran's simple view proved all too true and her husband began to die from the feet upwards. For no apparent reason he lost all strength in his feet, then his lower legs and upper legs. When it reached his torso he was admitted to hospital, discharged and re-admitted. I discovered that he had had a similar job to my father in the printing side of the newspaper business. A job which needed strong and dextrous hands. The strength of his hands became a watchword for us.

On the last day of his life I visited him in hospital. He was very weak but on hearing my voice he brought a fluttery hand from under the sheet and gave my hand a squeeze. He could no longer speak and I sat there holding his hand, wondering what to do in this large open ward with people all around. Then I thought, just because he can't speak I shouldn't be deprived of conversation. I would just have to guess what might be of interest and I began speaking. I laughed about our first meeting and thanked him for his tolerance; I talked a little about my father and my family connections with Ireland; I told him about an Irish doctor I shared my room with at the clinic and how he had opened my eyes to the richness of Irish culture and the profound influence it had had on Western culture generally. I then remembered a poem I learned at school when studying Yeats and most of it came back to me:

SAILING TO BYZANTIUM
I

That is no country for old men. The young
In one another's arms, birds in the trees
– Those dying generations – at their song,
The salmon-falls, the mackerel-crowded seas,
Fish, flesh, or fowl, commend all summer long
Whatever is begotten, born and dies.
Caught in that sensual music all neglect
Monuments of unageing intellect.

II
An aged man is but a paltry thing,
A tattered coat upon a stick, unless
Soul clap its hands and sing, and louder sing
For every tatter in its mortal dress,
Nor is there singing school but studying
Monuments of its own magnificence;
And therefore I have sailed the seas and come
To the holy city of Byzantium.

As I finished the poem and began talking of something else, Mr. Doran gave a violent shake of his arm, throwing my hand off. I suddenly felt that I had been imposing all this 'conversation' when perhaps he just wanted to get on with his dying. I took the hint and began to leave. Looking back I saw his hand fluttering again so went back and received the slightest of squeezes. The next day I rang his wife to find he had died that evening. She had been with him and she thought he had died peacefully. She said she had initially been worried about an occasional but violent shaking of his arm, but the doctors had told her it was a muscular spasm over which he had no control.

Some months later I made a long-promised trip with Mrs. Doran (whom I had not seen since her husband's death) to Regents Park, which she and her husband had visited regularly. Over three hours brisk walking on a beautiful autumn day she showed me every corner of the park. We finished with a walk round the Rose Garden, or as Mrs. Doran insisted, the Queen Anne Garden (it's official name), which was opened the day she and her husband were married.

TO BE OR NOT TO BE

At the day hospital attended by Mrs. Young was a man who suffered from acute wheezing bouts. He and his family were referred to the family therapy clinic and seen by the team's occupational therapist. Each time she brought up a subject which seemed to be to the point the man broke into a fit of wheezing. He was already overweight and the wheezing seemed to blow him up further, as well as turn his face purple. It was frightening to watch even from behind the one-way screen. In the same room there was little doubt that the man might die. The therapy was getting nowhere.

I rang through to the therapist and suggested she ask the man what arrangements he had made for his funeral. She thought the suggestion preposterous and did not take it up. The session continued to get nowhere. Later the therapist came out to discuss her frustration with the team. We had ideas about useful areas for discussion and this time I explained the reason for my question. The therapist agreed to ask it if the man had another fit.

When she broached his relationship with his elderly mother he began wheezing. When he stopped she asked him in a very matter of fact voice what arrangements he was making for his funeral. He and his mother were flabbergasted. The therapist went on to talk about how important funerals are and what a difference being prepared for them makes: cremation or burial, particularly special guests, people to be excluded, flowers or donations, financial provision. The family were still open-mouthed and when the man asked what she was on about, the therapist said that she assumed that he must have realised that any one of these wheezing attacks, given his age and weight, could give him a heart attack. She then asked him if he would like to use some time in the session to discuss the funeral. At this he became quite angry, declaring in no uncertain terms that he had come to talk about his weekend home with his mother and as he had no intention of dying this weekend could they get on with it. A variety of difficult and painful issues then came up for discussion and there was no more wheezing.

Very often if a client threatens us with his or her death we are at a loss: we don't want to give way to blackmail and we don't want not to take the threat seriously. I use the words 'threaten' and 'blackmail' in this context to describe our reaction to the client as much as the client's behaviour itself. I have often talked to people considering suicide or letting themselves die without experiencing any sense of threat or blackmail. Sometimes people feel that way and are secure enough to express it. But in other situations the suggestion of death feels like an attempt to somehow control others. The man just described seemed only to have attacks when the therapist raised issues he did not wish to address. The attacks made the therapist back off but in a way which left her feeling guilty and powerless – as if she had lost control of her side of the conversation. This feeling can be even more disempowering when someone threatens suicide – whole families can be held in thrall for fear of precipitating the deed. We have all heard stories about how someone said "Go on then, do it" and they all lived happily ever after; but most of us are too afraid to be part of a story with a different ending to adopt such a *macho* response.

The difficulty with suicide *threats* which by their nature are not intended to lead to death, is they may do just that if not responded to effectively. A threat ignored can lead to a suicide *attempt*. A suicide attempt not taken seriously can lead to another and when someone plays with death in this way, it is not too difficult to have an accident. On the other hand if the threat is taken seriously, it can seem like reinforcement. If each time the man wheezes the therapist (or anyone else) changes the subject, the man learns to wheeze even more until one day his heart gives up. Those around him are left feeling guilty that they did not tackle him more directly and also guilty that they did not avoid all difficult subjects. Everyone ends up a loser.

The 'funeral' question is a way of taking a suicide threat seriously without responding to the control or 'blackmail' element. If a person is seriously considering death, then it is only reasonable that they also consider the funeral. Discussion of the details makes concrete the therapist's belief in the seriousness of the threat, shows that the therapist is not frightened off by the thought of death and indirectly challenges the client to declare his or her real intentions.

Clients respond to the question very differently: some with amazement, some with anger, some with amusement and some with interest, but in all cases it leads to a removal of the threat.

Mr. Keeper took it wistfully. He was a man of seventy-five referred to me for depression. For the first half of the second session he went down and down, making several references to being better off dead. I began to feel put off my stride by these remarks:

Mr. K	I'm anti-life.
T	And when you want to live what is it that makes you want to live?
Mr. K	I'm not sure that I do want to live.
T	And if you did want to live what would be the things you would like to keep happening?

I am still at this point trying to work on Mr. Keeper's more positive side and for awhile this strategy works. He talks about his wife, children and grandchildren, but after a minute or two he sinks even further:

Mr. K	Sigh – It's better to die. Why not? Why?
T	Do you know what sort of funeral you'll be having?
Mr. K	Oh yes, a Jewish funeral – it's very basic, it's paid for, you pay for it all your life. You belong to a synagogue and they make the funeral arrangements. They give you this box which is very and extremely basic. You know, you see these Middle Eastern funerals and you see the raw box.
T	And who would be the chief guests at your funeral?
Mr. K	Oh, they'd all come. My daughters would moan me – I mean mourn me, and they've got hundreds and hundreds of friends. I mean my son-in-law when his mother died, he said prayers every night at seven or eight o'clock and they all came. All the mourners will come, it'll be crowds.
T	So it will be quite a funeral!
Mr. K	Oh, yes, and I even know what they're going to say.
T	You know what they're going to say?
Mr. K	Yes, they'll say: "He was inoffensive, quiet, wouldn't hurt anyone". I know that, I mean it's all the same stories they tell over the box.

T   And if they were going to tell a different sort of story
          what would they tell?

Mr. K   (*Thoughtful pause*) I wonder – couldn't come to grips
          with life I think.

T   Do you think so?

Mr. K   Certainly.

T   I'm not so sure!

Mr. K   I'm all the better for coming to see you!

By the end of this short discussion Mr. Keeper was noticeably
more cheerful and he never mentioned dying in the same way
again.

CHAPTER 8

A GOOD LIFE

FROM PROBLEM TO SOLUTION

Early in 1989 two colleagues[6] and I set up the Brief Therapy Project at the Marlborough Family Service. We had recently read a paper by Steve de Shazer and his colleagues at the Brief Family Therapy Center in Milwaukee, Wisconsin and were very taken with their ideas. De Shazer had written two recent books on a new approach to therapy which was switching attention from problem to solution. George, Ratner and I have written more fully about this work in *Problem to Solution* (1990). Here I will only outline briefly the main principles of this quite revolutionary approach to counselling. De Shazer's discovery was that understanding problems is not necessarily the best route to finding solutions. Indeed, it can even hinder the solution process. Taking the journey from London to Edinburgh as an example, a visitor unfamiliar with these countries, their geography and size, could be given precise directions which take him through every coastal town north of London. Eventually, after criss-crossing from coast to coast, gaining a great understanding of the terrain, the visitor would arrive at Edinburgh tired but informed – and quite oblivious to the oddness of the route. Another visitor might be given directions for the shortest route and arrive in Edinburgh several days before her counterpart, though much less knowledgeable about the geography of the two countries. Each would be satisfied with the journey in so far as they each understood it to be the best route. Only if they met and compared notes would they be in a position to reassess the wisdom of their respective 'choices'. Similarly, if a counsellor believes a problem is deep-seated and complex, then the route to its solution is likely to be complex and lengthy. And if a counsellor believes a problem is insoluble, then it is likely to be treated as such and so it may remain. Much of de Shazer's early work was around fitting solutions to problems, and it was while engaged in this that he

---

[6] Evan George and Harvey Ratner, both Senior Social Workers and Family Therapists at the Marlborough Family Service

began to notice that solutions seemed to have more in common with each other than they did with the problems they were solving. He found, for instance, that whenever a client began to notice exceptions to the problem, the problem itself began to lessen – this seemed to occur no matter what the problem was. Similarly, when a client did something different in relation to a recurring problem, the problem would lessen or even disappear – again this proved to be the case over a whole range of *different* problems. Once de Shazer and his team noticed this they began to study solutions – what works in counselling. This led to *solution focused therapy* in which a client's solution patterns are the subject of study, not the client's problems.

STEPS TO SOLUTION

Once a client has begun to talk about a problem, the counsellor's task is to find out those times when it doesn't happen – particularly the times when the client expects it to happen and it doesn't. These *exceptions* to the problem provide the key to a subsequent solution. In searching for them the counsellor has to listen very carefully to the client. If the client isn't ready to talk about exceptions but wants to expand further on the problem, this wish must be respected but not necessarily endorsed with problem focused questions. Eventually, exceptions will be found (in most cases anyway), and the counsellor spends as much time as possible finding out about their circumstances: what is *different* at the time the exceptions occur.

When the problem and its exceptions have been discovered, the counsellor can look to the future and establish *goals* – what will need to be achieved to bring the counselling sessions to an end. One way of doing this is to ask a variation of de Shazer's *Miracle question*: "If there were a miracle tonight while you were asleep (so you didn't know it had happened) and your problem were to disappear how would you know about it when you woke up? What would be the first signs?" This question leads to a detailed discussion of the behaviour the client will be engaged in when the problem is solved. It will include other people's reaction to the client and the client's reaction to them. The exceptions that have already been discovered can then be used as evidence that parts of the 'miracle' are already beginning to happen.

At the end of each session (usually after a short break for the counsellor to think about and digest the information provided) the client is complimented for whatever qualities, strengths and achievements have been demonstrated and then usually given a task. Often the task is simply to "notice the things happening in your life which you want to keep happening", which helps a client focus on exceptions. Sometimes a client does this so successfully the problem sinks into oblivion but, more often less dramatic results provide both the client and counsellor with further exceptions from which an eventual solution will be constructed.

Each session is spent searching for further exceptions, times when the client was successful in avoiding the problem or producing different behaviour. It doesn't matter if the exceptions are deliberately brought about by the client or if they come 'out of the blue'. They represent different ways of arriving at the same goal: a solution. As much detail as possible of the circumstances of each exception is sought so any successful behaviour can be repeated. One of the greatest values of this approach is the extent to which it relies on the client's own way of doing things. As far as possible the counsellor builds on what the client is already doing rather than making his or her own suggestions. The counsellor's role is to encourage as much talk about what is working as possible and to 'cheer on' anything the client does which appears to be successful – *if it works do more of it*. Sometimes, if a client is stuck in a repetitive cycle, then a more radical suggestion might be made. I was talking with a woman once who was in difficulties with her husband. I asked her: "What will be the first sign that your relationship is improving?" She said it would be when her husband made her a cup of tea. In all their married life he had never done this. I asked her to tell me when she would next be 'ordered' to make the tea. She said at four o'clock that afternoon. My suggestion was: "When your husband comes home from work and tells you to make the tea, instead of stopping what you are doing and making the tea, *do something different*, anything you like as long as it is different." That afternoon she had the first cup of tea her husband had ever made her and she anticipated many more!

A POSTCARD FROM BERLIN

When I first began using this solution focused approach I was a little over-enthusiastic, and the Berlin Wall still stood. One of my first clients was a Jewish Berliner who had survived the Holocaust and vowed never to go back, even though this meant forfeiting a German pension (which she said had to be claimed in Berlin itself). She had referred herself to the Institute of Family Therapy because she was estranged from her daughter and, at seventy-five, was worried about dying without a reconciliation. Her daughter had moved to the one place she could not go – Berlin – and had changed her telephone number to stop her mother ringing her. She was a wonderful woman with untold strengths and many achievements behind her. I was so impressed with these I barely noticed her impatience, and after three meetings she wrote to cancel the fourth thanking me for my positive outlook but saying that it was not at all helpful. I was very upset and contemplated returning to my more traditional family therapy past. I sent her a short note respecting her wishes and as an afterthought added: "If you ever get to Berlin, send me a card!"

Six weeks later I received a postcard from Berlin saying only: "All is well." My faith was restored! Since then I have learned to match my pace more to that of the client and to introduce 'solution talk' a little more gently.

MRS. GOOD – A CASE OF DEPRESSION?

The Referral

At about the same time Mrs. Good, aged 69 was referred by her G.P. for depression. She had suffered from bouts of depression all her life, usually in connection with family crises. This episode, however, seemed to have arisen without any obvious cause and was one of the worst she had had. The doctor had even begun to consider an admission to a psychiatric hospital.

First Exception

Because she sounded desperate Mrs. Good was seen within a few days. In the waiting room she looked very sprightly and cheerful – quite unlike her description of herself – and I decided to capitalise on this. My assumption was that it was important for her to 'keep her chin up' and not to let the world see how down she felt. I also thought that this might be one of the things which kept her going. That being the case, it was worth encouraging – it was an *exception* to the problem in so far as it was an aspect of her life, her appearance, which the problem had not taken over.

Mrs. Good   I don't know where to start, I just feel bloody awful, I really do.

T   You do a very good job of not letting it show, don't you?

Mrs. G   Make -up. I've got a birthmark on my face and that's something I simply have to cover. Even when I was in labour I did that and I think that helps to set me up.

T   In labour?

Mrs. G   Yes – I didn't want them to see my birthmark.

T   Because you looked very together downstairs and that wasn't just make-up.

Mrs. G   (*with enthusiasm*) Oh, that's great to know that then!

T   Oh, you looked ...

Mrs. G   I feel dreadful inside, absolutely awful.

T   How do you manage to keep up such a good show?

Here Mrs. Good is about to switch to problem-talk but I decide to hold this off a while longer. I do this largely because of her very enthusiastic response to my statement about her looking 'very together'. This endorses my view that looks are important and it also represents an exception itself: her tone of voice was far from that of a woman feeling depressed. Mrs. Good continues:

Mrs. G   God knows. But by the weekend I was absolutely shaking and I went to see my doctor and she said: "We'll have to consider putting you into hospital." I don't want to do that.

T   You're certainly...

Mrs. G   Clear-headed aren't I?

T   You're certainly clear-headed but you're also very good at getting people to take you seriously.

Mrs. G   Yes, when I phoned the doctor yesterday and told her
             I was going to the Marlborough she said: "What,
             already?" and I said "Yes, I arranged it myself." She
             was surprised I was seen so quickly.

T   Well, you were obviously very desperate and if
             someone is really feeling bad we try to see them as
             quickly as possible, and you were very good at
             putting your situation across.

Mrs. G   Thank you.

It was worth pressing on with the focus on exceptions. Though
Mrs. Good still stayed with the problem, she gave *herself* a
compliment and accepted one from me – that she knew how to get
people to take her seriously. These are all potential pillars for a
solution. At this point it is impossible to say which will prove most
useful but the more there are the more opportunities there will be.
With four strengths (her appearance, her ability to sound
enthusiastic, her clear-headness and her ability to get people to
take her seriously) identified within the first couple of minutes, I
then acknowledged the seriousness of her problem but still
without giving her an opportunity to discuss it at length. Before
doing that I want to draw out a few other strengths which are
becoming apparent and might prove even more useful.

Discovering Strengths

The session continues:

T   So let me tell you a little about what we might do –
             particularly with someone like you who is obviously
             one of life's survivors, if you don't mind me saying so.

Mrs. G   Yes, I had a doctor once who said I'd never break
             down – and I was going through another very difficult
             time.

T   So my view of you is – and I know I hardly know you,
             but from our phone conversation and the few minutes
             we've spent together today you are obviously
             someone who wants to get on with life.

Mrs. G   Oh yes, Oh yes – I don't want to give it up!

T   That you want to get on as quickly as possible.

Mrs. G   Oh yes, I want to get better and get better quickly, if that's possible.

Two more important strengths are now acknowledged – Mrs. Good's survival skills, for which there is the corroborative opinion of a past doctor, and her wish to get on with life. These represent a belief in the surmountability of problems and the motivation to do something about them – invaluable assets in overcoming depression.

The Problem

Mrs. Good then goes on to describe some of her life and her present feelings of awfulness. She has three children, all with children of their own, and also has two sisters with children. She has not had an easy life but she has certainly made the most of it and experienced periods of intense happiness as well as misery. The story supports everything that has already been defined in the first part of the session. When she has finished I begin to look for some goals.

The Miracle Question

T   Let me ask you a hypothetical question because it sounds as if you are waking up with a pretty gloomy view.

Mrs. G   Yes – it's absolutely dreadful (*goes on to describe a typical morning*).

T   You have a very clear view of this depression, which will be very useful when we want to look at it in more detail. But let's just say that in the night a miracle happens and this depressed feeling goes. When you wake up in the morning how will you know – how will you know? What will be different?

Mrs. G   I'd feel different inside me. I wouldn't have this dreadful despair.

T   Is it a physical or a mental feeling?

Mrs. G   It's both, I feel like cardboard in my chest (she further describes physical sensations in her chest and head).

T	So let's go back to this magical morning – what will be different that day?
Mrs. G	People – people.
T	Would that be people coming to you or you going to them?
Mrs. G	I don't know – I can't think at the moment. I just want to go out and have energy.
T	So if you had energy what would you do – you said you'd go out. What else?
Mrs. G	Go back to my old routine I suppose.
T	What would that be? What would your old routine be?
Mrs. G	Well, on Mondays my old routine was pension, paying the rent and shopping.

At first this did not seem a very fruitful search for a goal. Mrs. Good had great difficulty picturing anything in detail and could only talk generally of feeling less depressed and meeting people. It is eventually her desperation which provides the stepping stone: she says she wants to have energy and then can say what she would do with it. What she would do first is almost too mundane for her to mention, but it is exactly this mundane daily routine which will tell her that she is getting better. We go through the routine in as much detail as possible, partly to look for further clues and partly to help Mrs. Good become familiar again with the idea of the routine.

Staying Up

Mrs. Good then goes down into her problems again, this time going as far as pondering death. It is a serious thought.

T	It strikes me that there's a bit of you somewhere that would like to hang on and see what else life has to offer.
Mrs. G	Oh, yes, and I don't want to hurt people.
T	Because you are clearly a person who has led your life as someone with a future because you present as a person with a future.

Mrs. G   Yes, I'm the sort of person who likes to have
          something to look forward to – something to strive for
          – but at the moment there's nothing for me.
T   But you're striving – you're here so you are striving.
Mrs. G   But what for?
T   Would you do something during the week which I
          think will be helpful? It won't necessarily get rid of the
          cardboard in your chest or wire wool in your head but
          I think it will provide a useful start – a sort of
          foundation stone.
Mrs. G   Would you like me to take my washing to the
          launderette?
T   You're thinking exactly along the same lines as me!
          What I'd like us to work out is one thing for you to do
          each day between now and when we next meet –
          because I'd like to build on this capacity you have to
          keep life going even when things are full of despair
          and you are having to keep going in the dark because
          you're not a person who stands still.
Mrs. G   And I don't want to give up either.
T   No – that's quite clear. Let me tell you a story which I
          think you'll like.

The Monk's Tale

It is clear that Mrs. Good is not seriously considering suicide and
she accepts the definition of herself as a person with a future –
even if at present she cannot see what that future holds. In
reaching my suggestion before me, she is showing that she
already knows what the first steps to a solution are – that she
must re-establish the normal routine of her life. She must start
moving again even though she doesn't yet know where to.

The story is one I heard from Bill O'Hanlon, another influential
solution focused therapist.

In a monastery, high in the Himalayan foothills, the Buddhist
monks worked most of their lives to become initiated into the high
priesthood. Few achieved this most honoured position but all

strived to reach it. At least fifty years of intensive teaching, contemplation and preparation were required before the 'novices' could begin the ceremony and, though the monastery had no shortage of new monks, several years might go by before one successfully completed the rite of passage.

It was for this rite that the monks spent their fifty years preparing, yet it was something for which no preparation was possible. When a monk became ready he had only to enter a hitherto forbidden door. The door would close behind him forever. All he had to do was cross the room he had entered and leave through a door in the opposite wall. The room contained the physical, mental and spiritual embodiment of that monk's worst and most deep-rooted fear.

Many years had passed without a successful completion of the ceremony and the high priests were in much need of new blood. Our monk had been one of their favourites and they were pained to think that he too might be lost. It was because of his exceptional abilities and great youth (he was only sixty-two) that they decided to break their usual silence. The night before the ceremony the monk's own tutor, the oldest of the priests, came to him in his cell and gave him one small piece of advice: "Whatever happens when you pass through the door, keep putting one foot in front of the other; stop, and you will be doomed." The next day the High Priests gained a new member.

The aim of the story was to give importance to those very things Mrs. Good did to keep herself going and indirectly to encourage her to do more of them.

I finished the first session by asking her to try and do one small task each day during the following week.

The Second Session

She came back the following week:

Mrs. G   I feel so much better, you know, so much better!
T   That's terrific news, terrific news!

Mrs. G	I think you've helped me an awful lot because after last Wednesday I felt pretty grim, pretty awful I must admit.
T	Well, it was a gruelling session. We went through a lot.
Mrs. G	No, no, I think it just brought things forward and I called into a friend on the way home.
T	On Wednesday!
Mrs. G	Yes, on Wednesday, straight after I saw you. In fact I met her on the bus and she said, "You look a bit fed up, come and have a cup of tea." So I went with her.
T	That was a stroke of luck!
Mrs. G	It was, but I could only stay 10 minutes before I began to feel awful again so -
T	Ten minutes! You'd never have believed you could have stayed at all when we were talking last Wednesday.
Mrs. G	No, but I did and then I called on my neighbour to say I wouldn't be going to the tenants' meeting that night. Their daughter answered the door and she said, "Oh, Aunty Peg are you all right?" Such a nice girl. Anyway, half an hour later her father came up and said, "Come on, you're coming with us." So I went and sat with them for half an hour.
T	So you spent time with someone else as well.
Mrs. G	Yes, and I've done all the things you said and I went shopping on Thursday. It was like a nightmare but I did it. I thought of your Buddhist novices and that kept me going – sweat pouring down the back of my neck even though it was a bitterly cold night – and I got through it and felt so pleased.

Mrs. Good had obviously made great use of the first session not just by rebuilding some routine into her life, but also by noticing her small achievements as they occurred. Her meetings with friends and neighbours would no doubt still have taken place, but they would have served as evidence of her depression. She was now using them as a measurement of her achievement – being able to stay ten minutes or half an hour. It is just this switch of focus to *what is working* that provides the basis for rapid solution development and, indeed, Mrs. Good had made great strides:

Defining Progress

T	So you've been getting up to three or four o'clock in the afternoon without feeling too bad?
Mrs. G	Yes.
T	That's marvellous.
Mrs. G	Is it?
T	Yes, I certainly think so.
Mrs. G	I think so too!
	Honestly, I've been feeling pretty bad with indigestion and thinking I've got cancer, like my father. But then I thought it might be anxiety about coming here – not about seeing you because I've been looking forward to that, but anxiety about getting up in time.
T	But you managed it.
Mrs. G	Yes, I did and I feel quite pleased with myself about that.

Again, Mrs. Good is able to give herself credit and she has almost halved the amount of time she feels really low. But she is still very up and down and becomes very down as she tells me about having her handbag stolen. She sees this as an appalling reflection on human nature and considers whether it is worth living in this world.

T	I don't believe you when you say that.
Mrs. G	I'm pushing things away now – I don't want anything more to happen to me.
T	I'm sure you've had a hell of a lot worse things happen to you than having your handbag stolen.
Mrs. G	Honestly, you know it's an awful thing to say but I think I've had a hell of a life (Mrs. Good goes on to describe some particular incidents including an occasion when a counsellor said to her, "You've had such a sad life."). She had found this very upsetting and described it as a "stupid thing to say."

Family Matters

We go on to look at Mrs. Good's family by drawing a family tree and considering the qualities of each member and what their contribution has been. The family history contains many painful events, but also in Mrs. Good's terms "moments of pure happiness." She describes her family as a family of extremes with little in between, and I question this, suggesting that there are many gradations to be seen. She then says that she herself isn't extreme. This is useful because 'extreme' difficulties are seen to be the hardest to overcome. The less extreme Mrs. Good sees herself, the less difficult will it be for her to surmount her problems. She also describes very strong bonds between women in the family.

T   What you've described is a very strong family. An extremely strong family.

Mrs. G   (*pause*) Yes, because we are a family which communicates. My brother's wife phones me every day, and *everyone* tells me they love me (*she shows me a letter from her granddaughters, aged six and seven*).

T   There you are, you can see that trait (*the love and warmth expressed between the women*) passed on to a fourth generation – and how has it been passed on? Through you. You are the only woman in your geneeration, yet these are your mother's qualities coming through your grandchildren. You have a lot to be proud of.

Mrs. G   I have haven't I!

Though Mrs. Good describes a great deal that is good in her family, she also feels cut off from them and sometimes angry. It is not clear what the anger is about but she is keen to improve relationships. I therefore give her a number of tasks.

Firstly, I ask her to ask her sister-in-law when she phones up each day not to enquire about how depressed she is, but to ask what she has been doing which is good for her. This is an attempt to shift the sister-in-law's focus to solution building, which in fact misfires. The following session Mrs. Good brings with her a 'message' from her sister-in-law suggesting what we should be talking about in our meeting! It is Mrs. Good herself who finds the best way of convincing her sister-in-law that she is on the mend. She does this by going out for an evening. When her sister-in-law phones and receives no answer, she imagines the worst. She gets very cross with Mrs. Good, but it serves the purpose of reducing her worry and allowing her to think more hopefully of her sister-in-law's future.

The homework tasks which developed around Mrs. Good's two daughters had more effect. Out of a discussion about grandparents, parents and children and what they liked from each other, arose the idea that Mrs. Good write thanking her grandchildren for thanking them for their birthday letters, *and* her daughter expressing her appreciation for having got the children to write to her – the first letters she had ever received from them. Mrs. Good had taken such pleasure from her grandchildren's notes my idea was to help her generate a warmer relationship between herself and her daughter. It seemed likely that this would have a significant effect on her overall mood. The response to this task was a phone call from her daughter and Mrs. Good being taken for a day out with the family. Her daughter felt so warmed by the letter and Mrs. Good felt so warmed by her daughter's response that their relationship went into a dramatic upward cycle – they began to notice all the things they liked about each other and put to one side the irritations and dislikes, and their negative attributes diminished to unobtrusive proportions.

The third interactional task at the end of this second session was to do with Mrs. Good's youngest daughter Josie. Josie was the daughter with whom she spent most time and for whom she had the most negative feelings. She had spent several minutes describing how Josie couldn't look after herself and how her life was in a mess. She had always blamed herself for this and felt that she had particularly failed her daughter when she refused to visit her after Josie's third suicide attempt ten years previously. Mrs. Good said she had been unable to go through it again – the visits to the hospital, the pleading, the rows and blame – and had refused to respond to the phone call from the police: "She'll have to sink or swim on her own." Mrs. Good's view was that she had more or less sunk. While Mrs. Good still could not think of anything different she could have done the night of Josie's last suicide attempt, she still felt deeply guilty. It was this guilt which partly fed her negative view of her daughter.

In fact, the story of Mrs. Good's relationship with Josie could be seen in an entirely different light. Whatever part she might have played in the three suicide attempts her acknowledgement of her daughter's ultimate independence might have been the saving of her. Certainly Haley's view, as discussed in Chapter 5, would be that the suicide attempts were Josie's dangerous way of staying tied to her mother. In this context Mrs. Good's seemingly callous refusal to respond can be seen as a way of releasing Josie and allowing her to grow up. Since that time Josie had married, become a mother and lived a perfectly normal life. She had had very occasional trouble over bills and her husband had not always been in work but she was no failure.

This reinterpretation of Mrs. Good's 'abandonment' of her daughter was a great relief to her and set the scene for the third task. This was simply, on her next visit to Josie, to notice everything she liked about her.

The Third Session

By the third session Mrs. Good was holding off her depression until about six o'clock and had begun to read again. She had spent a weekend with Josie and had had a "marvellous time". She described how they had made up a bed for her with cushions on the sitting room floor and how she had felt "so cosy and secure". She seemed to have forgotten many of her previous complaints about Josie and spoke instead of what a lovely child her grandson was and of how Josie was turning out to be a good mother.

We had two more meetings, the fourth with Mrs. Good feeling worse in herself but this time not letting it stop from her getting on. She kept the picture of the Buddhist monk in her mind and kept going. We continued to look at the ordinary, practical aspects of living, as well as relationships with family and friends, and Mrs. Good went off with yet more homework tasks we had developed together.

By the fifth session Mrs. Good was feeling better again but had just had a liver complaint diagnosed. I suggested that this could well be the cause of her 'depression' since the liver has such a vital part to play in the interconnections between physical and emotional states. She hoped this was the case. She had been reading more and we returned the books we had borrowed from each other. We fixed a meeting for three weeks later but a few days before I received a message that Mrs. Good had been admitted to hospital suffering from the last stages of cancer. On the day of our appointment I visited her in hospital, but she had just slipped into a coma.

The End

Josie was by her bed and we spoke at length about her mother. She thought the world of her, as did all her family. They had discussed her meetings with me and had often laughed at my idiosyncratic ways and suggestions but Josie said the whole family had appreciated the sessions, because Mrs. Good had used them to get closer to her family. Their view was that at some level Mrs. Good knew she was going to die and wanted to set her house in order. The sessions had helped both to keep her going to the end and to reassess and reaffirm her most important relationships.

Mrs. Good died that evening.

Postscript

A year later Josie phoned me to ask if she could watch some of the tapes I had made of her mother. I could think of many reasons why not but none sufficient to overcome my instinct to say 'yes'. I edited some pieces which were likely to reinforce Josie's very positive experiences with her mother, and we sat together for three quarters of an hour watching them. It was during that three quarters of an hour that I decided to write this book.

FURTHER READING

Herr, J.J. and Weakland, J.H., 'Counselling Elders and their Families: Practical Techniques for Applied Gerontology' *Springer* N.Y., 1979
This is the only work I have come across on family therapy and older people but it is also very good. John Weakland has been one of the world's most influential family therapists and this book describes his theories more clearly than I have seen elsewhere. There are excellent and detailed case studies covering different sorts of problems, including confusion, intergenerational conflicts and loneliness. I have not seen it on sale here so you may need to order it from the American Publisher. Cost: £15-£25.

Skynner, A.R.C. and Cleese, J. 'Families and How to Survive Them', *Methuen*, 1983
This book by the first British family therapist and John Cleese (of *Monty Python, Fawlty Towers*, etc.) is currently the most popular family therapy book. It somehow seems to capture almost everyone's experience and has done more than anything to popularise family therapy. A good introduction and a good read.

Burnham, J. B., 'Family Therapy', *Tavistock*, 1986
For a more academic introduction John Burnham's book is excellent. He has been greatly influenced by the 'Milan group' a team of psychiatrists from Milan who have been one of the most influential forces in family therapy over recent years.

For a more 'advanced' introduction, the best book available is Hoffman, L., 'Foundations of Family Therapy' *Basic Books*, 1981.

Minuchin, S. and Fishman, C., 'Family Therapy Techniques', *Harvard*, 1981.
This is an excellent account of structural family therapy, clearly written and quite inspirational in its effect. Each technique is illustrated with extensive transcripts of family interviews and most readers develop Minuchin's Argentinean accent before completing the book!

Haley, J., 'Leaving Home', *McGraw Hill*, 1980.
One of Haley's many books. Haley, too, is a founding family therapist and his books are always well written and provocative. This is ostensibly a book about young adults in psychiatric treatment but it has far wider implications.

George, E., Iveson, C. and Ratner, H., 'Problem to Solution: Brief Therapy with Individuals and Families', *BT Press*, London, 1990.
A short and, most people say, very readable account of brief solution focused therapy with four extensive case studies and their transcripts.

de Shazer, S., 'Keys to Solution in Brief Therapy',
Norton, N.Y., 1985
de Shazer, S., 'Clues: Investigating Solution in Brief Therapy',
Norton, N.Y., 1988
These two books outline the work of de Shazer and his team. Extremely clear and well written they formed the basis of the Brief Therapy Project at the Marlborough Family Service. For a shorter version of this approach de Shazer and his team have written the following paper:

de Shazer, S.; Berg, I.K.; Lipchick, E.; Nunnally, E.; Molnar, A.; Gingerich, W.; and Weiner-Davis, M. 'Brief Therapy: Focused Solution Development', *Family Process* 25, 207-222, 1986.

Another excellent book on solution focused work is
O'Hanlon, W.H. and Weiner-Davis, M., 'In Search of Solutions', *Norton*, N.Y., 1989.

There is a great shortage of family therapy literature in relation to older people, which means that most of it is still to be written. Over the past few years I have met a number of specialists in work with older people who could begin filling the hole, so start looking out for some interesting books.

One of the best book shops for Family Therapy literature is Karnac who have branches at:
118 Finchley Road, London NW3 (071-431 1075)

56 Gloucester Road, London SW7 (071-584 3303)

They are both knowledgeable and helpful.

Other books quoted are:
'The Diaries of Jane Somers' by Doris Lessing, *Penguin*, 1985.
Originally, Lessing wrote this anonymously as two books in part to see to see how difficult it is for an unknown author to be published. It is quite different from Lessing's other books, and is a moving and sometimes inspirational account of the life of an older person and the professionals who surround her.

'The Name of the Rose' by Umberto Eco, *Picador*, 1983.
One of the most popular books of the past decade – a 'who dunnit' with philosophy, religion and history in equal measures. A very good book for 'meaningful' quotations!

'The Collected Poems of W.B. Yeats', *Papermac*, 1982.